God Spoke Tibetan

The Epic Story of the Men Who Gave the Bible to Tibet, the Forbidden Land

by Allan Maberly

Evangel Bible Translators
PO Box 669
Rockwall, TX 75087-0669
(469) 480-8519

www.evangelbible.org

Library of Congress Catalog Card No. 77-82034

ISBN 0-9712249-5-1

Printed by:
St. Francis Press
St. Benedict Road,
Ernakulam, Cochin - 682 018
India

Chapter illustrations by Robert Edward Tretheway

About This Book and Its Author

Most of us would expect the story of a Bible translation to be covered with a layer of scholarly dust and sprinkled with split hairs left over from semantic fine points. With the Tibetan Bible, however, all the reverse is true.

Who, for example, would imagine a Bible translation set in motion by the assassination of a Dalai Lama within the walls of forbidden Lhasa? Who would expect the mere printing of a Bible to run up against a Himalayan thunderstorm, the unbelievable heat of the Indian plains, the bombs of Adolf Hitler, a shooting war over Kashmir, and an avalanche? What other Bible translation ever required *ninety years* of heartbreaks to complete?

Who could foresee that a new Bible ultimately would result from the hairbreadth escape of a Tibetan government official, accused by a lamaist sorcerer of a crime he did not commit? Or that a centuries-old Tibetan book discovered in an isolated monastery would provide the key to the completion of God's Book in a new language?

Who, finally, could foresee that the Christian Scriptures in Tibetan would be in immediate demand by the government of Communist China?

Allan Maberly, the author of this book, is a native of Sydney, Australia. He spent eight years in the Himalayas as a medical missionary. From their home in Kalimpong, Northern India, he, his wife, and three daughters looked out on five countries—India, Tibet, Nepal, Sikkim, and Bhutan. They lived almost in the shadow of

Kanchenjunga, the world's third highest mountain. Maberly learned to speak both Nepalese and Tibetan and made a special study of those countries. He became a good friend of Sherpa Tensing Norkay, famed guide of the Hillary Everest expedition.

Foremost among the author's sources for the story was the late David McDonald, who lived in Kalimpong. McDonald, son of a Scottish trader father and a Tibetan mother, lived all his life near the Tibetan frontier and spoke Tibetan from early childhood. He was personally acquainted with many facets of this story and was one of those who checked the Bible manuscript. Maberly interviewed him for days, taking copious notes and learning facts he would never have gained otherwise. Maberly has also drawn on *The Story of the Tibetan Bible*, a brochure by Canon Chandhu Ray published by the British and Foreign Bible Society; and an article, "Bible No. 188," in *Christian News Digest*. In addition, the author gathered information and ideas from others who had to do with the actual production of the Bible.

Maberly's personal library includes a sizable collection of books on Tibet and the Himalayas. These, together with his own travels in southern Tibet (he was never able personally to enter Lhasa), have given him insight into the exotic culture, customs, and psychology of the Tibetans.

Lesser details of the story recounted here, gathered from so many sources, sometimes differ. For example, some have reported that a careless Indian post office employee spilled water on the manuscript proofs. Another version has it that a mountain storm destroyed the proofs. Mr. McDonald personally told Maberly about the mountain storm and what it did to the Bible and saddlebags; the author has therefore adopted the McDonald version. These details, of course, do not affect the overall truth of the story. Spellings of Tibetan words also vary: Gappel is also spelled Gappal, Gapel, and Gallap. To some, *tsamba* is *tsampa*; *rimpoche* is also spelled *rinpoche*. Again, these things are of little consequence.

For the chronology of his narrative, Mr. Maberly has carefully researched the Tibetan calendar and reconciled it with the English one to the satisfaction of several authorities. The years of the Wood Hare, Fire Dragon, Water Dragon, Fire Dog, and the rest—all are authentic.

Details aside, the author has given us the unique story of a great task carried out by heroic men. They struggled against unbelievable, even superhuman odds—against "the rulers of this present darkness, against the spiritual hosts of wickedness," of which the apostle Paul speaks.

Which is the greater miracle: the divine intervention that made possible the Tibetan Scriptures, or the power inherent in those Scriptures that constrains men to do the difficult, even the impossible, as here recorded? Read *God Spoke Tibetan*; then try to decide for yourself.

Contents

Foreword

By Rev. H. Syvelle Phillips

In early 1976, I resigned from the church I had pastored for many years and set about to organize the missions ministry that is now known as Evangel Bible Translators. From the beginning, the basic purpose of this new organization was to translate, publish, and distribute God's Word for people who had never had the Scriptures in their own language.

A few days after my farewell service at the church, I received a message from a family that had been very much a part of our ministry for a number of years. The father of the family had died, and they requested that I conduct his funeral.

While waiting in the chapel for the final arrangements to be made and the funeral service to begin, I met and visited with Reverend George Vandeman, a relative of the deceased, who had also been asked by the family to participate in the funeral service. For many years, Rev. Vandeman had presented a powerful television broadcast entitled *It is Written.*

While we waited, Rev. Vandeman and I shared a time of fellowship. He was curious as to why I would leave the church and start a new missionary organization.

I welcomed the opportunity to explain that God had sovereignly called me to encourage an interest in Bible translation among Christians to whom I had the opportunity to minister. This call had become my vision and the passion of my life. To provide the leadership necessary for this Bible translation ministry, I had to make a choice, as I could not both lead the missionary ministry and pastor a church. I chose to give myself, wholly and without reservation, to the challenging effort of organizing and leading Evangel Bible Translators. With joy and enthusiasm, I shared what I knew to be the will of God for the rest of my life. Suddenly he said to me, "There's a wonderful book that you must read. I will send you a copy."

In a few days, a beautifully bound book entitled *God Spoke Tibetan* arrived in the mail. I found it so fascinating that I could not put it down. I read into the wee hours of the morning and simply could not tear myself away from this interesting and provocative book. Little did I realize that this book would have a vital part in my future ministry. Neither did I realize that God would use the story contained in it to mold my life, to touch the lives of thousands of people, and to enlighten many people to what it means to be a Bible translator. The task of translation is enormous and difficult, but we also see the ultimate triumph of giving the Scriptures to a people, in their own tongue, for the first time.

After many years, I continue to see the profound impact of this story on the ministry and development of Evangel Bible Translators. I see how *God Spoke Tibetan*—a book that came into my hands as a result of what I thought was a casual conversation—has helped to mold and chart a course for my life.

Those who do missions work recognize that Tibet is one of the most resistant countries in the world to the Gospel of Jesus Christ. Evangelizing the Tibetan people and establishing Bible-believing churches has been exceedingly demanding and has challenged the Church in a severe way. To this day, very little progress has been made. There has been little encouragement for those with a burden and a concern for Tibet, yet there is evidence of divine activity. God is answering the prayers of the millions of people who have taken the spiritual needs of the Tibetan people into their hearts and have committed themselves to aggressively intercede for this land that is held in the grip of demonic power, fear, darkness, and superstition.

Revelation 11:15 says, "And the seventh angel sounded; and there were great voices in heaven, saying, The kingdoms of this world are become the kingdoms of our Lord, and of his Christ; and he shall reign for ever and ever." (King James Version) That process is underway; the kingdoms of this world are becoming the kingdoms of our God and of His Christ, and Tibet is included in God's grand scheme for reaching all men with His redemptive grace. There are Tibetans who have been redeemed, who have fought the good fight and kept the faith, who have committed their lives to God and who have paid an enormous price to be Christians. There will be Tibetans around the throne of God worshipping the Lamb who was slain for their redemption.

I was enthralled by *God Spoke Tibetan*. I found it to be one of those stories that simply cannot be put down once you start reading. This book so clearly and powerfully portrays the struggle and the triumph of those who endeavored to give God's Word to people for the first time, that I knew I needed to give copies of it to my friends. I hoped that they would understand the cause to which I had committed my life and that they would come to share my vision. Quite frankly, I also hoped that they would join me in prayer and contribute financially to this new missions endeavor.

I began by buying a dozen copies of this book which I gave to friends. I then bought a hundred. Before long I had purchased 500 and had ordered more, only to be told that they were out of print, so I made arrangements to have them reprinted. Soon it was being widely circulated among people that I knew well.

After sending a copy of *God Spoke Tibetan* to Pat Robertson, founder of the *700 Club* television ministry, I was invited to appear on the program to tell this wonderful story in my own words. I was very busy in those days, but I took pride in my ability to manage my calendar, be punctual, and keep appointments. Somehow though, I had overlooked the date that I was supposed to be in Virginia Beach to appear on the *700 Club*. To my utter astonishment and horror, I discovered at noon one day that I was to be in Virginia Beach at 8:00 the next morning. I was in southern California and there seemed to be no way to get to Virginia Beach in that timeframe.

My staff and I stopped what we were doing and called every airline. Without exception, every staff member came to me and reported, "Pastor, it is impossible. You cannot get to Virginia Beach in time to appear on the *700 Club* in the morning at 8:00." But I could not give up. I said, "Route me anywhere—Canada, Mexico, whatever it takes—get me to Virginia Beach."

Then God gave me an idea. I remembered that my friend, Bob Smith, in Birmingham, Alabama, owned a manufacturing company that had a corporate airplane, and

I felt free to call on him to help me. I called and told him I was in trouble, and he asked what he could do for me. I told him that I was embarrassed to tell him, but I had missed my flight and needed his plane to meet me in Atlanta the next morning at 4:00 (I had checked with Delta Air Lines and found a red-eye from Los Angeles to Atlanta) and take me to Virginia Beach. He said, "Our company plane flies on company business every day, but amazingly, tomorrow it is not scheduled to fly. The pilot is standing by waiting for me to give him instructions. I will call and tell him to fly to Atlanta in the morning."

He made arrangements for us to meet, and at 4:00 the next morning I jumped off the big jet, hailed a cab to take me to the other side of the airport where the private plane was waiting, boarded, and off we went to Virginia Beach. I arrived at the *700 Club* with ten minutes to spare. I never told Pat Robertson or Ben Kinchlow (the host of the program) what a mistake I had made. Somehow God helped me to be fresh and alert and able to tell the story. I then went to the hotel and collapsed!

I had no idea of the importance of my appearance on that television program or what was riding on my being able to tell this story. Later I came to understand that the devil knew the importance of my being on that show and what would happen as a result of my being there. I believe that is why I had such difficulty getting to Virginia Beach on time.

Viewing the program that day in upstate New York was a Mrs. Miller, who had served as a missionary on the Tibetan border for forty-plus years. She had retired back to America and was watching the *700 Club* that morning. A few days later I received a letter from this veteran missionary requesting a copy of *God Spoke Tibetan*, which I gladly sent. After reading the book, Mrs. Miller wrote me again, saying that she thought she knew the descendants of Yoseb Gergan, the man whose story is told in this book. She told me, "I am going to do the detective work to see if I can find his descendants."

Several months passed and I received yet another letter from Mrs. Miller telling me that she had found Yoseb Gergan's grandson, Elijah Gergan, and that he was a seminary student in South Korea. She gave me his address and I immediately wrote to him. We began to build a friendship by correspondence, and I invited Elijah to come to southern California and be a guest in our home. He is exceptionally bright, very sharp and an outstanding Christian with a beautiful, wonderful spirit. Our family quickly came to love him. In fact, our young sons wept when Elijah left because their hearts had been knitted to this special man of God—a native Tibetan and descendent of the man who was, as far as we know, the first Tibetan to ever become a Christian, and who would later be used of God to write a Bible for his own people.

Elijah told us during this visit that he knew that his grandfather (pictured on page 90) was a Bible translator, but he knew little else. He welcomed this book about his grandfather and sent a copy to his father who was then working as a professor of Tibetan History and Culture at a prestigious university in Germany. The father said that the information about Yoseb Gergan was amazingly accurate. We, of course, were pleased by this confirmation of the book's accuracy.

Because of the testimony written in this book, our conversations with Elijah, and because of his knowledge of the spiritual needs of the Tibetan people, Elijah made a commitment to God and to us to continue the work that his grandfather had begun in 1855. That was a marvelous step forward for the cause of Christ in Tibet.

Elijah returned to northern India, where he lives on the border of Tibet, to minister to the Tibetan people living in that vast region. There he helped Evangel Bible Translators spearhead an effort to reproduce the New Testament and to produce an Old Testament in the Tibetan language.

Later, Elijah married Meena, the daughter of a Nepali who was involved in translating the Bible into one of the Nepali languages. I told him that his children were destined to be little Bible translators, because that seemed to be a family heritage!

While speaking at a missions convention in Florida, the host pastor asked me to tell about Tibet and the story that is in this book. In the congregation was a delegation of ladies who had just returned from a missions trip to Haiti. (I learned later that they came to the service rather reluctantly, because they were exhausted, and felt that the last thing they needed to do was to go to a missionary service.) I shared about what God was doing for Tibet and what He was doing in my life in regards to that land. I did not realize at that time that these ladies had an intercessory prayer group that was dedicated to praying for Tibet and had been interceding for many years on behalf of the spiritual needs of the Tibetans. They were very enthusiastic as we chatted after the service about their concern for Tibet and our ministry's commitment to see that the Tibetan people would again have a Bible in their own language.

A few days later, after reading *God Spoke Tibetan*, the ladies requested a copy of the Tibetan New Testament. At first I refused to send it to them because I had what I thought was (and probably still is) the only copy of the Tibetan New Testament in North America. I teasingly said to them, "If I loan you my precious book you will probably spill gravy on it." We laughed about it, but I eventually sent it to them, and they did proceed to spill gravy on my treasured book!

They were very mysterious about why they wanted this New Testament. I knew that they could not read it, so why would they want a Tibetan Bible? They called again, still very mysterious and secretive, and asked, "Where is the Gospel of John in this Tibetan New Testament?" I told them that I could not read Tibetan and could not tell them.

While I was talking to them though, it occurred to me that in the pages of *God Spoke Tibetan*, John 3:16 is printed in the Tibetan script. I said, "I think if you take the book and carefully match its text with the text in the New Testament, you will be able to locate John 3:16, and once you locate this verse, you can very easily identify where the Gospel of John begins and ends."

Weeks went by and another call came saying, "We thought you would like to know that we did find the Gospel of John in the Tibetan New Testament and we have taken it upon ourselves to print 5,000 copies of the Gospel of John, and we are going to take them to Tibet." Because they could only carry 4,000 copies into Tibet, they would send me the remaining 1,000 copies.

I responded, "You can't go to Tibet. Tibet is closed." (China was very closed at that time and no one was being allowed into Tibet.) I repeated, "You can't go there."

They replied, "Well, we did not know that, so we prayed over three members of our group, and they left yesterday to go to Tibet." A few weeks later they told me the happy story of how they succeeded getting into China and making their way across the country into Tibet where they delivered those 4,000 copies of the Gospel of John.

In this book, you will read about the printing of 5,000 copies of the original and only edition of the complete New Testament in Tibetan. As far as we knew, all copies had been distributed and no more were available.

To get 4,000 copies of the Gospel of John into Tibet, a land closed and forbidden, was a major achievement. We later learned that these ladies, in their zealous and simple approach, had gone to Buddhist temples. They noticed that the monks who were spinning prayer wheels and burning incense would remove their chiffon orange-colored outer robes and hang them in what we would call a cloakroom or closet at the entrance to the temple. The ladies would slip into the entryway and put copies of the Gospel of John into the pockets of the robes while the monks were praying in the inner part of the temple. When the monks came out from their prayer time and put on their robes, they found this strange book in their pockets.

These ladies had a wonderful time distributing the Gospel of John in Tibet, and the authorities never stopped them. That in itself was a wonderful miracle. We rejoiced with them at the progress being made through their dedicated efforts to get the Gospel of John into Tibet for the first time since 1949. I wondered though what I would ever do with the 1,000 copies of the Gospel of John that they had sent to me.

Meanwhile, I appeared as a guest on *100 Huntley Street*, a Canadian television program much like the *700 Club* in the United States, and had been asked to tell this story. This led to a friendship with one of the interviewers and her husband, a newscaster stationed in Jerusalem.

One day while at Evangel Bible Translators' missions orientation school in Wisconsin, I received a call from this newscaster. He told me, "I have been employed by the United States Chamber of Commerce and the Chinese government to take a delegation of VIPs and business leaders from America into China, and we think there is a very good possibility that we may get to go to Tibet. I remember the story you told when my wife interviewed you. I read the book that you gave her, and I was just wondering if there are any copies of the Gospel of John or New Testaments in the Tibetan language that we could take with us. My television crew will be traveling with this group of VIPs. Because we are guests of the communist government of China, we will not be examined too closely at the border, and there is a good chance that we can get gospel literature into China along with our cameras and television equipment."

In the meantime, I had been to India and had met again with Elijah Gergan. Riding in a taxi in Bangalore, we saw the Bible Society's warehouse. I asked him, "I wonder if, by chance, any of the original 5,000 New Testaments printed in Tibetan so long ago could be stored away somewhere in the Bible house." Elijah went into the Bible house and inquired, but they told him that there were no Tibetan New Testaments there and if any of the original 5,000 remained, they would be in their warehouse in Calcutta.

A few days later we were in Calcutta. Elijah went to the Bible house, and again was told there were no New Testaments in Tibetan. Elijah asked the manager, "Would you please give me your permission to go into the warehouse and look to see if I can find any of these New Testaments that were printed in 1949? You know, they could have been here so long that they could have just been lost, and you might not even know what a New Testament in Tibetan looks like. If you would be kind enough to let me go look, maybe I could find some." The manager gave his permission for Elijah to go in and look around. He found 1,100 of the original 5,000 New Testaments stored in there where they had been for over forty years.

We made arrangements to buy all of these New Testaments, which were still in good condition. I then had in my possession 1,100 complete New Testaments in Tibetan to go along with 1,000 copies of the Gospel of John which were in California. I also had a television crew volunteering to take these precious books into Tibet. (When I say that I had these New Testaments in my hand, that is not quite accurate. We knew where they were and we had control of them, but they were still in Calcutta.)

I learned that my newscaster friend was traveling from Israel to Canada. From there he would go to San Francisco, to Hong Kong and then into Tibet. By the time I learned of his trip, he was already flying to Canada. I had to somehow arrange for the Gospels of John that were in my office in Orange, California to meet his plane in San Francisco and get the 1,100 New Testaments from Calcutta to Hong Kong. I worked all night by telephone, calling my friends in Hong Kong and India. I asked that they help me get the New Testaments on a British Airways flight leaving Calcutta that night and arriving in Hong Kong in time for them to be transferred to my friend and his television crew.

The Evangel Bible Translators staff in California succeeded in getting the Gospels of John to San Francisco, where the television crew picked them up and took them on to Hong Kong. My friends in Calcutta were also able to deliver the 1,100 New Testaments to Hong Kong. This television crew, that I have never met, packed the books in with their gear and were able to get them across the border into China and on to Tibet where they delivered them.

Later I was told that as they were about to cross into China, the president of the Bank of America picked up the suitcases containing the copies of the Gospel of John and transported them across the border. When God summons a porter he sometimes chooses the most unlikely person! It was a wonderful victory for all of these Bibles to be brought together and successfully smuggled into Tibet.

Sometime later, I was in a hotel in Dallas, Texas eating lunch when a well-dressed lady came over to my table, introduced herself and asked me if I was Syvelle Phillips, the founder of Evangel Bible Translators. I told her that I was. She also asked if we had ever provided any Scriptures for the Tibetans. She went on to say, "I went to China a few weeks ago as a tourist, and at the last minute I was permitted to go into Tibet. While in Tibet, we visited the Buddhist temples. There we found copies of the Gospel of John in the hands of Buddhist priests who were reading them avidly. I know they were well-read because they were dirty and showed signs of having been used." This was a wonderful confirmation to me that these New Testaments and the Gospels of John had been successfully delivered to Tibet. They were now being read by the monks who spin the prayer wheels in the Buddhist temples. This was a great victory.

I received a letter one day from someone in Australia whom I did not know. He explained to me that his forebears had served for over forty years as missionaries, living in a valley in Tibet's extreme eastern corner. They had returned to Europe old and exhausted and had lived only a few more years.

Before their passing, they had sent a written history of their work in Tibet to their descendants, who were then living in Australia. They told of some very important documents stored in a trunk in the basement of a house in a remote part of Tibet. The letters authorized the descendants to retrieve these documents if the old missionaries themselves were unable to return to Tibet. The family members were intrigued. They wondered what was in the trunk, and wrote, asking if I knew anyone in, or associated with, Tibet. Only God knows how they got my address.

I responded by giving them Elijah Gergan's address. They contacted him and sent him copies of the letters that their missionary forebears had sent to them.

Taking these letters authorizing him to retrieve the contents of the trunk, Elijah traveled with his father to a remote Tibetan valley, where they introduced themselves to the owner of an ancient house. They showed her the letter, and she readily agreed to let them retrieve the trunk and its contents from the basement.

This trunk, which had been there for well over forty years, contained a hymnbook and five handwritten Tibetan New Testaments that were leather-bound and carefully preserved. Amazingly, there were no stains, no mildew, and no worm damage. These documents were all in excellent condition.

As Elijah and his father visited with the elderly owner, they learned that she was moving from her home because of her age and health. Within the next two weeks the house would be torn down. God's timing is always precise!

Later, when I was back in India, Elijah brought me a copy of one of those handwritten New Testaments and gingerly laid it in my hands. I held it, stared at it in awe, and asked Elijah, "What does it mean for us to find these handwritten New Testaments that have been written in yet another Tibetan dialect?"

(This was a dialect separate and distinct from the main Tibetan language. Apparently, these missionaries had written a few verses each day as part of their daily devotions. We believe they labored about thirty years writing these New Testaments. Each member of the family had handwritten his own copy. These Bibles were stored in a trunk, and God had supernaturally preserved them all of these years, and there I was holding one in my hand asking Elijah what it meant.)

He said, "It means that another language group in Tibet has a Bible written in their own language and it is available to be printed."

For many years, through our ministry, a Persian scribe prepared these manuscripts to print yet another Tibetan New Testament. God supernaturally preserved these hand-written copies of a New Testament for another language group that we knew nothing about.

I made another appearance on a television program, this time in El Paso, Texas, to tell this story again. When it ended, one of the technicians came to me with tears streaming down his cheeks and said, "I know what you are saying is true, because I worked in that valley installing a telephone system for one of the World Bank organizations, and I met the descendents of the converts of these old missionaries." He was rejoicing.

Later, I received a letter from Paul Coffman, a friend for many years, who was a veteran missionary to Asia and the founder of Asian Outreach. Paul's parents had been missionaries to Tibet, where he had grown up. By now, he was old and wanted to make a sentimental journey back to Tibet. He and a Chinese evangelist made the journey looking for the church that his father had built. He found nothing—no Christians, no fruit of his father's ministry—he felt very discouraged and melancholy that he could find no results of the many years of his parents' work. Suddenly, he heard one of the members of the delegation cry out in excitement. On a mountaintop overlooking Lhasa, the capital of Tibet, was a huge cross. They climbed to the top of this mountain and discovered that the cross had been anchored in cement.

Paul believed that this cross was a powerful silent witness to the fact that there are Christians in Lhasa serving the Lord in underground churches. Erecting the cross would have required a considerable number of people and would have been done at great risk. Apparently, to honor the Savior they had come to love, they were willing to risk their lives.

While this story that began in 1855 is not complete as Tibet remains in the grip of the forces of darkness, progress is being made. Elijah Gergan is now the pastor of a congregation of more than 200 believers and he runs a Christian school attended by more than 1,400 children. There are orphanages and schools in northern India and Nepal that minister to the needs of Tibetan children. Thousands of Christians now travel to Tibet each year to participate in intercessory prayer walks to witness and distribute Christian literature

The love and concern that has been expressed for the people of Tibet will not be in vain. The prayers being offered to God on behalf of this dark land will be answered. The sacrifice of missionaries, Bible translators, and those who invest time to take the Gospel to a people who live in spiritual darkness will be honored by our faithful God.

My prayer is that as you read this true story, God will put in your heart a love for the Tibetan people and a passion to help make Jesus known in this mysterious land. This drama will conclude with millions of Tibetans standing with the redeemed as we worship the Lamb of God.

Rev. H. Syvelle Phillips is the Founder and President of Evangel Bible Translators.

1/Death in the Palace

Slate-colored clouds scowled over Lhasa, Tibet's mysterious Forbidden City. A northeasterly wind whipped across the city and through the cobblestone streets making prayer flags flutter on the housetops and bells tinkle on the golden temple roofs. Intermittently the gods of the air hurled down fistfuls of hailstones, peppering the Potala—the thousand-room stone palace of the Dalai Lama—and the lesser buildings below it. The sun had made a few attempts to break through the overcast that day, then had wrapped itself in the blanket of clouds to keep out the chill wind.

On this blustery day, the last of the Tibetan year of the Wood Hare (1855), the Tibetans had completed plans to welcome the year of the Fire Dragon starting the next morning. Pilgrims from far-off icy plateaus and sheltered valleys in the Himalayas mingled with citizens of Lhasa in the crowded streets. Thousands of red-robed priests, spinning prayer wheels as they walked, joined with pilgrims from the provinces of Kham and Amdo to the east, and from Mongolia, Nepal, Sikkim, and Bhutan.

Resplendent images, freshly gilded for the ceremonies now beginning, glistened in the light of myriad butter lamps on the altars. Yak-butter images bigger than man-size, stained with bright colors for their single day of glory, stared unseeing from their temporary thrones. Incense rose in clouds from the temples, its pleasant aroma mingling with the acrid smell of burning butter, the odors of open drains, and the scent of people never known to bathe or wash their clothes.

A pilgrim from eastern Tibet, his leathery brown face framed by shaggy black hair under a fur hat, trudged wearily along the cobblestone pavement. He clutched tightly at his sheepskin coat as a malevolent gust of wind seemed determined to tear it from him. Suddenly he shuddered, but not from the raw weather. Rather, the cold hand of a nameless dread tore at his heart and made him shiver uncontrollably.

A few moments before, he had passed through the gateway under the giant *chorten*, the Buddhist shrine that guarded the entrance to the city. In a state of ecstasy at having arrived at this most sacred of all places, he had stopped an aged lama to inquire where the Presence would bestow his blessing.

The lama, busy spinning his prayer wheel and chanting, looked annoyed at the interruption. "The Dalai Lama is dead" he snapped, and resumed his chanting.

The pilgrim staggered as if struck by a blow.

"Dead? Dead, did you say?" The pilgrim peered anxiously at the old monk, who seemed to be back in a state of trance. "You mean the Dalai Lama, the incarnation of the great Chenresi, has left us? Tell me, it's not true, is it?" He clutched the lama's robes. "What has happened, venerable one?"

The old monk looked up again. The pilgrim saw that his eyes were filled with tears. Momentarily he stopped the chanting but kept the prayer wheel whirling. He began to speak.

"He was so young—only eighteen years of age. Yesterday he blessed the lamas outside Norbulingka, his summer palace. Did I not pass by and get his blessing?" The lama paused as he seemed to be reliving the moment when he had felt the touch of the tassel, bestowed by the Dalai Lama in blessing.

"Today he was to appear before us all at the Potala to welcome the new year and bless the pilgrims. But he departed in the night to the heavenly fields. I tell you, stranger, Chenresi would never just leave us like that. He was murdered."

Choking back a sob, the monk lapsed back into a state of trance and resumed his monotonous chanting. *"Om mani padme hum. Om mani padme hum"*—the age-old prayer of Tibet—"Hail, thou jewel in the lotus; hail, thou jewel in the lotus."

The pilgrim sighed deeply. Not knowing what else to do, he stood watching the old monk. But at last the monk staggered off along the sacred Lingkhor Road, leaving the pilgrim in stunned silence. Then the pilgrim noticed that a group of Khamba nomads had paused to listen to the monk's story.

"Let me get my hands on the villain!" A swarthy tribesman fingered the sword hanging from his belt. "I'll slit him from end to end and toss his remains in the Kyi Chu River!"

His companions murmured approval, adding their own imprecations upon the unknown scoundrel.

Just then an official in richly brocaded uniform paused beside them, listening to the tribesmen's threats. Seeing him, the tribesmen made a hissing sound to show their respect.

"The Oracle will soon find the truth," the official promised. "There is to be a séance tonight to find the wretch who committed the murder. Just find him, and we will do the rest!"

The official passed along the street, and the tribesmen resumed their discussion of the latest rumors.

The pilgrim had dragged his way across the towering Tibetan mountains, struggling over steep passes, invoking his gods as he came. At night he had shivered in his sheepskin robe, so inadequate in that icy waste. Before innumerable shrines he had added his meager offerings—a pinch of barley flour, a little salt, a bit of coral, or a lock of his own hair—while praying for strength to finish his pilgrimage. When weariness overcame him and the cold numbed him, thoughts of arrival in Lhasa, the Sacred City, revived him. Soon he would kneel before the Dalai Lama and receive the touch of the sacred tassel at the end of a wand. The thought brought an inner warmth to his body

and inspired him to press on with his pilgrimage. Now the
Dalai Lama, the supreme god of all Tibetans, was dead—
murdered.

The Tibetan Council of Ministers, the *Kashag*, had met
in session in a special room of the Potala since early
morning. Before the council, with its four members—
three laymen and a monk—sat the Regent, an old man of
dignified bearing who had governed Tibet until the Dalai
Lama came of age. His hair was coiled in a topknot and
fastened with a heavy jeweled clasp. A long jade earring
dangling from his left earlobe revealed him to be a noble
of the highest order. Tempu Gergan, Tibet's minister of
finance and one of the council members, addressed the
Regent.

"Hourly the crowd grows more impatient. Soon it will
take justice into its own hands. I need not remind you
what that means to us. Ever since the Eleventh Presence
came among us we have been responsible for his care."

Glaring at the old man, he continued, "You have acted
as Regent during the years of Dalai Lama's minority. Ab-
solute power rested in your hands for the control of Tibet.
Then the Presence ascended the throne, taking from you
and us the power that was ours. Will not the mob suspect
us members of *Kashag*, as they did when the Tenth Dalai
Lama was murdered?"

As minister of finance, Tempu Gergan held one of the
most coveted positions in Tibet. As a member of a noble
family he was respected for his wisdom as well as his position. His richly brocaded gown, tied with a bright sash,
showed him to be a man of wealth. The long sleeves fal-

ling almost to his knees set him apart as one who need not use his hands to earn a living. But of what use now was his wealth or noble birth if the mob should accuse him or his fellow members of the *Kashag* of the murder of the Dalai Lama, their god?

Again the council members recited the facts, as they had a dozen times. The boy king had occupied the throne only a few months since his eighteenth birthday. With dignity he had taken up the sacred office, administering both religious and secular affairs. Only the day before, he had held an audience for the priests from the huge Sera Monastery. Then that morning his monk attendant had screamed from the sacred bedroom that the god lay dead. No doubt a visitor had slipped poison into the lama's butter tea. A physician-lama from Chapokri Monastery rushed in to minister to the boy, but too late. Even now the sound of the wailing chant of the monks, with clashing of cymbals, echoed along the palace corridors as the death ritual began.

"We must find the Mongolian!" The Regent settled back on his deep cushions. "He was the last one to visit the Presence. The Mongolian begged for an audience with his holiness last night, and it was granted. The attendants in an outer room heard his holiness intone a blessing on his visitor. Shortly afterward the hermit rushed from the room, past the guards, and vanished. Without question, he is guilty, but where is he?"

The monk member of the *Kashag* spoke up. "All is arranged for the Oracle to invoke the gods tonight. Then we will know the truth. I believe this hermit was the villain, but was he only a paid agent?" Turning to Tempu, he glared unpleasantly, "Tempu, *your* name has been whispered!"

Tempu felt the blood drain from his face. "But that's impossible. Why should *I* commit such a vile deed?" He turned to the other members for assurance, but they merely shrugged. Then they arose and left the room.

For a few moments Tempu sat numbly trying to think. "Me? A suspect? That's impossible! I had nothing to do with this at all. Yet, what would happen if the Oracle should name me?"

As the enormity of the accusation dawned on him, he felt faint and dizzy. But he must think clearly. Ever since he had accused the present Oracle of being unreliable, he had been out of favor with him. The Oracle had condemned other innocent men before; yet the people still blindly believed him. Again Tempu shuddered. First there would be hideous torture for him, then he would be sewn alive into a yakskin and thrown into the river—that is, if the Khambas didn't get him first. It was too horrible to think about. He must be ready to escape if necessary.

He clapped his hands, and a servant entered the room. Crouching low, the servant poked his tongue out in respect.

"Did you call me, master?"

"Yes. I have work for you to do. Call my steward Kenchung to come here immediately. See that you talk to no one else of this business."

"*Laso, laso* [Yes, yes]. I am going now."

Slowly a plan formulated in Tempu's mind. He would escape from Lhasa before the net closed. Speed was vital, and he must use all his ingenuity to bring it off.

The steward came in, looking bewildered at the hasty summons. Tempu felt it best to place the problem clearly before him. "Kenchung, I have been warned that I may be accused as the murderer of the Dalai Lama. You know what that will mean!"

"You? That's impossible! Name the scoundrel who would blame you for this crime, and I will deal with him."

In spite of his bravado, Kenchung was visibly shaken by the news. He knew that no one was more respected in Lhasa than his master, but he also knew that one of the members of the *Kashag* would be the prime suspect. The monk minister was unlikely to be implicated, so that left only three and possibly the Regent.

"What can we do, master? Can you pay the Oracle sufficient to clear your name?"

"No, that won't help. You know he is no friend of mine. We must make plans to leave Lhasa in an hour."

"But that's impossible. Where will we find yaks and mules? And if we do find them, what should we take and where could we go?"

Tempu held up his hand for silence. "No one must know our real plans. Kampashung, a trader from Nepal, has just come in with a caravan. I hear he is looking for a return load. Go and hire his mules and yaks, but don't look too eager. Just tell him you have an important trading mission in Bhutan and must leave in an hour. On no account reveal the real purpose of our plans. Our lives depend on your silence. You will need to prepare our most trusted servants to go with you. It is already late in the day."

"*Laso, laso*. I will do my best." Kenchung nodded and

left quickly to arrange for the caravan.

As Tempu slipped out of the Potala a few minutes later, he felt, more than saw, the angry eyes of the mob. They pressed in threateningly around him, but a monk guard stepped up and took him by the arm. Shouldering aside the crowd, he commanded, "Down, you swine! Make way for his lordship. Must he walk over all the carrion in Lhasa to leave the palace?" With a heavy cane he cleared a way for Tempu to pass through the hostile mob. More than once Tempu winced as he heard his name spat out by nomad warriors.

"Have you found the culprit yet?" The monk guard looked anxiously at Tempu.

"Not yet, though we know it must be the Mongolian hermit."

Tempu found his home in turmoil. The servants, he learned, had chattered busily about their master in his absence. Had he gone crazy? Why would he leave on a trading trip during *Losar*, the ten-day feast? they wondered. Anyone knew it was not auspicious to start a trading trip until the year of the Fire Dragon had been welcomed. And if this was a trading trip, why pack so much food? The servants could make no sense out of the furtive packing going on behind locked gates. Still their job was to obey, so they worked on.

Droma, Tempu's young wife, met her husband at the door. Kenchung had simply told her that her lord was going on a trip and preparations must be made. But she was suspicious. Intuition told her this was something more urgent than a trading trip. Now as she heard the news, she collapsed onto the nearest cushions.

"What will you do, Tempu? Where will you go?"

Tempu gazed into the deep brown eyes of his lovely wife—one of the most beautiful women of Tibet. She had been reared in luxury by wealthy parents, never knowing hardship. Quick-witted and cultured, she lived in the center of Lhasa's social world. How could he take her out onto the interminable bleak plateaus and across deep gorges with churning white rivers? Yet what other choice did they have?

"Maybe we will not need to flee, but we must be ready. You will go with Kenchung and the animals west along the Kyi Chu River and press on quickly south. You must get as far as possible from the city before night falls. There must be no dallying on the way; every mile is vital. If I am named, I will try to join you later. If my name is cleared, then a servant will be dispatched to recall you to Lhasa."

"You are not going, then?"

"Not yet. The *Kashag* will meet again this evening before the Oracle calls the gods. If I do not attend, they will be sure I am guilty and will send a party searching for us. We must have time for the pack animals to get well away."

"Isn't it dangerous to go back to the Potala?"

"It's dangerous whether I go or stay. I still hope the Oracle will name only the Mongolian." Wearily he turned to supervise the servants' work.

"What about money?" Droma wanted to know. "And must I leave all my furniture?"

"Don't worry about money. I have arranged ten mules with gold bars and three with silver. It is hidden in bags of salt, which have already been sent ahead. The mules are waiting just beyond the city wall. Leave the furniture as it is here, but pack plenty of skins and woolen clothing. You will take your jewelry also. You must disguise yourself so that no one will know you are a noblewoman. Go with Kenchung when you are ready. I have to leave at once for the meeting of the *Kashag*."

The *Kashag* conference dragged on for hours, but decided nothing. The Mongolian hermit must have escaped from the city; no one had so much as a clue. The decision now rested with the Oracle. Wearily the *Kashag* members left their council chamber late in the night and entered the temple room where the Oracle was to reveal the mystery.

Tempu stared at the Oracle's throne, where sat Nachung Choje, the religious master of Nachung Monastery and Tibet's state prophet. Two religious emblems flanked the throne: a trident bearing a clay model of a human skull, and a spear with a triangular red pennant attached. Below the spearhead a padded ring of material with three human eyes embroidered, glared at the spectators. The Oracle wore the heavy ceremonial robes of his office. On his right hand glittered the silver oracle ring; on his left wrist was the red-demon noose. An apron patterned with dragons covered the top half of the brocade gown that fell over his gold-trimmed boots. A massive helmet of silver and gold crowned his head. The helmet's circlet was embellished with five human skulls. The Oracle had his legs planted far apart, while his hands rested on his knees. His face looked tense. He breathed slowly, with eyes closed.

A high lama, an open censer in his hand, stood in front of the Oracle wafting the aromatic smoke of burning juniper branches and incense into the seer's face. Behind him rows of maroon-robed priests chanted in rising and falling cadence. A *rimpoche*, or living Buddha, sat facing the Oracle. He chanted an invocation, ringing a small hand-bell with the left hand, and with his right waving the sacred thunderbolt—*dhorje*. He was calling the tutelary divinity, the three-headed, six-armed Pehar to leave his celestial throne and hasten to receive the offerings laid out for him on the altar, then to take possession of his servant.

"Come hither, mighty Pehar, mighty thunderbolt. Take the *tormas* of meat and blood; the wooden platter with flour and butter; the human skulls with drink offerings—beer of Tibet, tea of China, sour milk, fresh milk. Accept the inner, outer, and secret offerings. Fulfill the duties imposed upon thee; reveal the future, disclose false accusations, protect the pious. But most important of all, tell us who slew Chenresi!"

Tempu's breath seemed to be choking him. Hot and cold shivers ran up and down his spine. He felt sick and faint as the tempo increased. The tempo of the chant also affected the Oracle. His head swayed this way and that as he greedily inhaled the incense. The yellow butter lamps on the altar flickered dully through the clouds of juniper smoke. Before the altar stood the figures of the priests, grotesque shadows in the dim light.

The penetrating odors and the shrill tinkle of the bell pressed in on Tempu's ears till he wanted to scream, "Stop! Stop!" But a hypnotic spell kept his eyes on the Oracle.

Now the clashing of cymbals and the throb of the great drum began to accelerate the chant of the priestly choir. The Oracle swayed and quivered. His facial muscles twitched. He bit his lower lip in a paroxysm of pain. Several times he lifted his hands as if warding off some malevolent power. His rapid breathing, keeping time with the chanting, changed into a hectic panting. Rivulets of sweat poured down his sallow face. The movements increased to continual spasmodic jerks. Startled, Tempu noticed that the face of the Oracle had undergone a terrifying change. It was no longer the face of the priest of Nachung, but the leering face of Pehar. The whole head seemed swollen; the skin changed to a dark-red color; the thick blue lips flecked with foam. Saliva dribbled from the corners of his mouth, now drawn down in an expression of cruel contempt.

The priest, now fully demon possessed, let out a scream. He leaped off the throne and began a slow, macabre dance. Seizing an offered sword, he grasped both ends and twisted it as if it were a piece of paper. Blood dripped from his clenched fist, which he slowly opened to let the twisted sword crash to the floor.

The watchers sat enthralled. "He has come! Pehar has come!"

The chanting died away as the Oracle wolfed down the meat offerings. With a grunt he seized a bowl made from a human skull and drained the potent drink offering. Now the *rimpoche*, with reverently bowed head, moved forward and placed a ceremonial scarf around the Oracle's neck. The act of veneration was not directed to the Oracle himself, but to the deity now occupying his body.

Tempu stood there cold but perspiring. His heart thumped so loudly he wondered if his companions could hear it. Yet he still hoped that Pehar would declare him innocent. He glanced around, looking for an escape route. Seeing all eyes fixed on the Oracle, he slipped toward a side door where he could watch proceedings from behind a protecting pillar.

Now the Oracle made strange gurgling sounds as if choking. The *rimpoche* began his ritual questioning.

"Has Pehar been well cared for?

"Have the monks been faithful in providing meat and drink offerings?

"Has the god had a safe journey from the heavenly fields?"

A monk scribe jotted down the cryptic answers from the Oracle. Many of the replies seemed unintelligible, but the scribe wrote on. At last the crucial question comes. Every ear strains to hear the *rimpoche* question the Oracle.

"Your Lord Chenresi has just departed his human shell to return to the abode of the gods. Tell us, why did he do this?"

The eyes of the Oracle opened for a moment and swept the room with a horrible stare. Tempu felt the ground sway around him as the eyes seemed to pause for a moment and bore into his soul. Then the eyes passed on and the lids fell over them again. The Oracle lapsed into incoherent muttering; then words began to form. "I see a golden cup with a demon dancing on the brim."

"Ah, the poison cup," someone whispered; but he was hissed into silence.

"There is a strange priest offering the cup to Chenresi.

He wears a high-peaked hat and tattered garments—"

Relief flooded over Tempu as he heard the Mongolian monk described. The Oracle had paused for a moment, but now continued: "I see around the holy one bags of gold and silver. A hand offers the silver to the strange priest— The face—the face—I cannot see the face— Yes, it is coming—"

Tempu's breath seemed to be choking him, while his legs felt as if they would collapse. He knew instinctively whom the Oracle was about to name. He flung himself out the door and fled down the passage. Pausing for a moment in a small room, he discarded his rich brocades and strode on as a peasant pilgrim. But even as he started again he heard a chorus of voices rising to a crescendo: "Tempu Gergan is the man! Seize him!"

He wanted to dash away madly, but he fought the mounting panic. He must look like a poor pilgrim. Would these eternal stairs never end? Would someone recognize him? It seemed hours since he had left the séance, but in fact only a few seconds had passed. At last he was clear of the building, heading toward the city wall. Now they were taking up his name as the story spread that Tempu Gergan had hired the Mongolian to commit murder. He knew the guards in the Potala would be frantically searching the thousand rooms for him. Any moment they would find his discarded clothing and know their prey had escaped. He must hurry!

Suddenly he heard a shout behind him, "Block the stairs. No one must leave the palace!"

He had escaped just in time. He dared not go to his home. Silently he slipped over the city wall where Choni, a trusted servant, waited with two horses.

"Quick, they are coming after us!"

Tempu Gergan flung himself onto the horse's back, grasped the mane, and spurred to a fast gallop along the road leading east toward China. A backward glance showed the flames rising from his burning house, tingeing the surrounding buildings with angry red in the gray pre-dawn darkness. In the glare of the fire he saw a group of horsemen galloping out from the city gates.

"Ride for your life," Tempu shouted, "or we are doomed!"

Glancing backward, he could see his pursuers coming on relentlessly.

2/The Gods of the Chang Tang

Ahead, just beyond the main ford of the Kyi Chu, lay a grove of willows stretching down to the river. If Tempu and his servant could reach the shelter of the trees, they had a chance to lose their pursuers in the gray half-light. As the two fugitives dashed up the riverbank, they were momentarily hidden from the shouting soldiers. Savagely Tempu swung his horse off the road into the sheltering willows. Before his horse had stopped, he leaped into the first large tree he found, then whipped his riderless horse along the trail again. He could hear his servant crashing through the undergrowth, dragging his horse out of sight.

They were not a moment too soon, for as Tempu's horse galloped off along the trail the horsemen flashed by. Tempu and his servant leaped on the hidden horse, recrossed the trail, and moved quickly along the riverbank. The horse, a large bay, snorted in protest at carrying two riders on his back, but he managed to maintain a steady canter. They headed for a little-used ford across the Kyi Chu River, which foamed between banks of gray granite.

Several miles west of Lhasa the fugitives recrossed the Kyi Chu River where it curved to the south. Here the road from the city divided, one road leading south toward India, the other stretching across the Nyenchentangla Range toward the bleak Chang Tang plateau. They took the northern road. Soon they left the main road and took a trail which followed a turbulent mountain stream up a narrow canyon. The steep canyon walls kept pressing them toward the swift current, but they gave the horse his head and let him follow the trail.

On the afternoon of the second day the fugitives found that the trail left the stream and climbed steeply toward a snowy pass. The freshly fallen snow muffled the hooves of the bay stallion as he struggled up the trail. The horse was having trouble keeping his footing, so the servant slipped to the ground and floundered along behind.

As they climbed the trail the wind grew stronger. When they reached the top of the pass, the gale forced them to seek shelter behind a rocky outcrop. Tempu stamped his feet wearily to restore circulation. Even now he was not unmindful of the gods of the Chang Tang into whose domain he was intruding. Bending down, he felt for a loose stone to throw on the votive cairn that marked the top of the pass. Hurling the stone through the air, he called on the gods to guide their way and confound their enemies. With a final shout to the gods the two men bowed their heads to the wind, now become a snowstorm, and pushed painfully forward.

"We shall need the gods tonight, master," shouted Choni above the fury of the wind.

"They will have a search party all through the mountains," replied Gergan, "but perhaps they will not venture far into the Chang Tang on a night like this. Only fools like us would venture into this demon-infested wilderness. And if they do follow us, the snow will cover our tracks."

Choni's only reply as the two men stumbled along on the far side of the pass was to chant the traditional prayer of gratitude to the plunging horse,

> *"Kyan-la mi chi-na, ta omen;*
> *Turl-la mi papna, mi-men."*

"If you do not carry him up the hill you are no horse;
If you do not walk down the hill you are no man."

The trail began to level out as the fugitives neared the edge of a vast plateau stretching to the west. In summer, nomads grazed their sheep and yaks on the short, thick grass that covered much of this area. The *kulgars*, or wild asses, roamed through the valleys unafraid of men, who respected their right to live. But now, near the end of winter, heavy snows covered these grazing grounds. Few nomads would be found in the hills now, as they moved to the lower valleys for the winter.

"Master, we must find shelter for the night," Choni urged. "We cannot go far tonight. You mount the horse again and let him have his head. With the help of the gods we will find shelter soon."

They stumbled on in the darkness, tripping over rocks and floundering in drifts. At last the horse pricked up his ears and whinnied, then turned off the trail into a ravine that offered some protection from the storm. For a moment both men feared they had stumbled into a hidden camp. They listened for human sounds, but heard only the moaning of the storm.

"Get a light, Choni. There may be shelter near here." Tempu slid off the horse and brushed the snow off his coat. Choni struck his flint, sending a shower of sparks into a handful of dried moss he had pulled from the folds of his voluminous robe. Blowing carefully on the smoldering moss, he was rewarded with a flicker of flame.

Protecting the flame from the wind, he held it above his head. In the instant before the light was snuffed out, he saw a small cave in the side of the ravine. Tempu now pulled a pine stick from behind the saddle and began to whittle slivers with his knife. Coaxing a flame to life, they ignited the chips, and with the flickering light they discovered a heap of yak dung to burn. How good it felt to warm their frozen bodies by the friendly flames.

From the saddlebag Choni took a small kettle in which to heat rancid butter tea. Never had they enjoyed the warm brew more than that night on the frozen Chang Tang. Mixing *tsamba*, roasted barley flour, with the scalding tea, they prepared a nourishing meal.

"A thousand curses on the Oracle!" muttered Tempu. "May the demons of Topla curdle his blood! May his lying tongue rot in his mouth!"

"Where will we go now, master?" Choni heaped another handful of dung on the fire. "Where is Kenchung, your steward, with the caravan and the mistress? Are they not headed south toward Bhutan?"

"Yes, but that was only a blind. Kenchung was to turn west and follow the Tsangpo River toward Tashi-Lhunpo. He was to follow a little-used trail above the pilgrim road."

"How will we find them now?" Choni wanted to know. "Is there any way across this wilderness? I have heard that demons roam these hills in winter."

Both men shuddered and moved closer to the fire. Tempu stared into the flames for a moment before replying.

"There is a chance we will find a nomad camp. Some of the nomads stay in the caves through the winter months. If we can get a guide and a couple of good yaks, we may break through to our families. If not—" He shrugged. "Hobble the horse, and let's crawl into the cave for the night and try to get some rest."

The gray dawn was a welcome sight to the fugitives who had dozed fitfully in the cold.

"Have you oats for the horse, Choni?"

"Not much, master. If we don't find the nomads and get food, the horse will perish in this cold."

"It won't only be the horse!" Tempu wondered if they really could hope to survive the Chang Tang wastes.

Soon they were on their way again. Where the trail leveled enough, they both rode; but more often they took turns trudging behind the horse. As far as they could see to the west, a white wilderness stretched before them without a sign of human dwelling. But eventually, far off to their left, they saw a wisp of smoke curling into the morning air.

"Look, master; there's fire over there."

"Yes, Choni; but how do we get over to that valley?"

"I think the trail winds over that way. We shall be able to see from the pass ahead."

As he plodded on, Tempu worried about his wife and the caravan. Could they have reached the mountains before the search party moved on their trail? Would he ever see them again? It was all in the hands of the gods; what was to be, would be, and nothing could change it. Every man must follow the fate marked for him by the stars. Had not his mother told him of ominous signs the day he was born? A crow had picked the eyes out of a newborn calf, and the sun had set bloodred. "Trouble," the old lama had muttered as he had consulted his charts. "This boy will know real trouble!"

"Yes," mused Tempu now. "Trouble has indeed come—and how bitter!"

At last the fugitives stumbled into the nomad camp in a sheltered valley. The nomads had pitched their tents below a rocky shelf adjoining a series of shallow caves in which their animals were sheltered. The tents were woven of yaks' hair; the natural greasiness made them quite waterproof.

The two men knew the nomads would be suspicious of strangers; only robbers or fugitives would venture into the Chang Tang in winter. A shaggy mastiff came charging toward them, snarling; but one of the nomads lunged for the dog and with difficulty restrained him.

"We are pilgrims and have lost our way," called

Tempu. "May we rest with you awhile?"

The nomads surveyed the visitors for a moment and, appearing satisfied that the men were harmless, beckoned them to come. As they entered the main tent, Tempu poked out his tongue in respectful greeting to the old nomad who sat on a saddle pack before a yak-dung fire. A wall about three feet high, built of dried yak dung, stood around the inside wall of the tent. This admirable arrangement worked both as a windbreak and as a handy source of fuel.

After long formalities, lubricated with copious draughts of butter tea, the men finally got down to business.

"You say you are a pilgrim?" The old nomad paused in his noisy drinking to survey his guest. "But pilgrims don't travel this way. And your horse looks quite fresh. You look more like an official to me."

His disguise must not be so good, Tempu thought. He must be careful. Leaning forward, he hissed in respect to the old nomad.

"Really you are very clever. I am a government official on a special mission. We are traveling this way to avoid suspicion. Can you help with yaks and guides? We will reward you well."

The old man still seemed suspicious, but at least, he said, this government official wasn't demanding compulsory animals—*ulag*—and food in his traveling, as the nobles usually did. So it was settled. A guide would take them through the hills, though the journey would be difficult. The next morning at first light they would leave with four yaks for baggage and riding. Tempu's horse was to be given to the nomads as part of the bargain; it would never survive the trip over the high passes ahead.

Tempu felt more hopeful. "Even yet we may succeed," he confided to Choni.

Farther south, Kenchung the steward hurried with his yak and mule caravan west along the Tsangpo River. He was apprehensive, wondering what had happened to his master. If Tempu Gergan's name had been cleared by the Oracle, they would have known long ago. But no news had come, and this could only mean that the master had also fled. They must push on rapidly to the secret rendez-vous near Tashi-Lhunpo. Droma, Tempu's wife, rode to-ward the back of the caravan, following the servants and most of the animals. They left the main trail and climbed into the mountains where the snow lay heavy. The family priest took care to propitiate the gods at every step. His prayer beads slipped rapidly through his fingers while his spinning prayer wheel ground out the eternal *"Om mani padme hum."* When they came to a *mani* wall they passed on the left to ensure favor from the gods. At every pass they invoked the gods of the mountains to care for them.

Kenchung was anxious to know what had happened in Lhasa, but he dared not question passing nomads. It would be three weeks before he could reach the agreed meeting place just north of Tashi-Lhunpo. The caravan was up and away before dawn while the snow was frozen hard. By midmorning the sun turned the valleys into stoves as the hot rays deflected off the miles of snow. Early each afternoon the sky would darken over with storm clouds laden with hail and sleet. The lumbering yaks could travel only a few miles each day when the weather was favorable, but slowly they moved toward the agreed meeting place.

Spring weather brought the thunder of avalanches as the snow melted on the higher peaks. Here and there a patch of green showed above the frozen earth, providing food for wild asses and antelopes. Nomads drove their flocks into the high pasturelands. Far below in the valley, the mighty Tsangpo River foamed milky white with melted snows as it rushed toward the gap in the Himalayas to flow on as the Brahmaputra River of India and finally empty in the Bay of Bengal.

In a secluded valley in the mountains, Tempu Gergan sat with his wife and servants recounting what had happened in Lhasa. Was it really only a month since he had fled from the city? The nightmare trip over the Chang Tang had lasted, it seemed, an eternity. How thankful he had been to find his wife and the caravan waiting for him when his plodding yaks crested the last pass. Now he hoped he might settle in Tashi-Lhunpo. He had had enough of travel.

From here the trail dropped swiftly to the river, where travelers ferried over in yak-hide coracles. Traders and pilgrims flowed into the city of Shigatse, just beyond which lay the temple city of Tashi-Lhunpo. Almost as famous as Lhasa for its golden temples and magnificent images, the city was revered by every pilgrim to Tibet's holy places.

Tempu sent Kenchung with two other servants to determine whether they might safely enter the city. "What news from the great city?" Kenchung casually asked the first trader he met.

"They are still mourning the death of the Presence. In fact, the ceremonies will continue another thirty days while they place his embalmed body in the hall of the gods."

"Have they found the culprit yet?"

"The Oracle revealed that it was Tempu Gergan, one of the chief councillors; but he fled from Lhasa before they could lay hands on him. Hundreds of soldiers are searching for him, and there is a price of a thousand silver *gormo* on his head." The trader leaned closer to Kenchung and spoke in a low voice, "It is rumored he is somewhere in these parts and may try to enter the city. So the whole place is swarming with soldiers. Wouldn't I like to get my hands on the villain. A thousand *gormo*—it's a fortune!"

Kenchung had heard enough. The caravan was in immediate danger, so they must clear the district at once. But where could they find safety? The whole country was in an uproar over their escape. Many hinted that Gergan was in league with the devil, who had spirited him away to safety. Kenchung felt that the only hope was to move back into the hills and follow the Rako Tsangpo River toward the west. If they could reach Kashmir, they would be safe.

When Tempu heard the news, he wondered how he could endure any more travel. Perhaps they should rest a few days before moving on. But thoughts of rest died quickly.

"Master, come quickly!" One of the servants peered anxiously down into the valley and pointed his finger.

"Look! A party of mounted men!"

One look revealed that the soldiers were fully armed and moving rapidly. In less than an hour they would overtake Gergan's caravan.

"Quickly! Strike camp! Choni, you take the sheep and half the yaks and head westward along the ridge. Kenchung, you take the mules and move north back toward the Chang Tang. The mules will move faster without the yaks. I will take the rest of the caravan and head northeast. If we are surrounded, we must fight it out."

As the caravan fanned into the hills, they heard the shouts of the soldiers as they urged their mountain ponies up the trail.

3/"Om Mani Padme Hum"

"The dew is on the lotus – Rise, Great Sun!
And lift my leaf and mix me with the wave.
Om mani padme hum, the sunrise comes;
The dewdrop slips into a shining sea."
-Edwin Arnold, The Light of Asia

Looking backward, Tempu Gergan could see the soldiers climb the valley slopes until they crested the hill and galloped up to the recently vacated campsite.

Fortunately, at this time Tempu's party caught up with a large caravan carrying salt from the Tabia-tsaka lakes some thirty days' travel to the northwest. Some two hundred yaks made up the caravan, and they raised an enormous cloud of dust. Tempu's party mingled with them and continued along the trail. They were greatly relieved when their lookout reported that after the soldiers had approached the salt caravan, they had apparently decided not to pursue anyone farther and returned toward the city. Tempu Gergan sent scouts to gather his scattered caravan and push on steadily to the west.

Day followed day as the caravan plodded on across the desolate Tibetan steppes. They met few nomads, as they had left the main migratory routes. Fording innumerable rivers, crossing steep passes, they battled with the elements and occasionally met with robber bands. The robbers, seeing the party well organized and armed, moved on to easier prey.

To the south the snow-clad Himalayas stretched along the horizon like a string of pearls, caressing the heads of the lower mountains. With great excitement the fugitives approached the most sacred spot in all Asia, Kailas, *Kang-Rimpoche*, the "ice jewel" of the gods. Like a gigantic *chorten* of the gods its hoary peak points up to paradise where Tibetans believe myriad gods sit enthroned in unfathomable space. From the highlands of Kham in the remote east of Tibet, from Naktsang and Amdo, from Bongba, from the black tents which stand like the spots of a leopard among the dreary valleys of Tibet, from the Ladakh valleys in Kashmir, and from the Himalayan lands in the south, thousands of pilgrims come annually to pace slowly, in deep meditation, the twenty-eight miles of the sacred ring road around this navel of the earth, the mount of salvation.

What tremendous merit could be obtained by walking that sacred road! Tempu planned to spend a week here following the pilgrim path and doing obeisance at the many *gompas*, or monasteries, set like precious stones in a bangle around the base of *Kang-Rimpoche*. Was not man bound to the wheel of life passing through lives innumerable in the quest for salvation? Each life added another drop to the ocean of eternity, but could it ever be enough? Fate decreed that birth and death, suffering and pleasure, each would come in its appointed time. *Karma* was everything. Man could not change the course of his life, but he could seek for merit.

"Ah, it was an evil day when this soul found this body." Tempu stood gazing at the sacred massif while his men bowed in worship. "Can there be no release from this miserable life of suffering? Come, Droma, let us begin our pilgrimage. Who knows but that the gods may yet hear us?"

With prayer wheels and prayer beads in their hands they set out on the sacred road of salvation. Some pilgrims painfully crawled the distance on their hands and knees. Others measured the distance with their own bodies, prostrating themselves along the path. Now began the steep zigzag in the troublesome path among the steep boulders. On every rock they found pebbles heaped in offering to the gods to gain merit for the one who lifts yet another stone out of the path of the following pilgrims. They saw horns and bones deposited in large quantities— gifts to the gods who guard the pass.

At the halfway mark, Droma plucked a black strand of hair from her head and pressed the hair into a smear of butter she carried with her. Placing this on a huge rock where pilgrims without number had performed the same ritual, she bowed her head in worship. Droma swung her prayer wheel vigorously, joining with Tempu in the ever-lasting dirge of Tibet: *"Om mani padme hum. Om mani padme hum."*

The wind blew gustily from the breath of the gods on the glacier of Kailas. Droma shivered, but not from the cold.

"Om mani padme hum. Om mani padme hum."

Key between the visible and invisible, between the real and unreal. Mindful of the things which can never be secured in this life. What is life anyway? The sparrows chirping on yonder temple wall are not sparrows at all. They are guardian spirits. And the flames that flicker before the sacred image in the sanctuary—are they really flames? Does anyone know what a flame is?

"Om mani padme hum. Om mani padme hum."

The alpha and omega of life. As closely connected to the land of the snows as buzzing bees to the hive, as the flutter of prayer banners on the pass, as the ceaseless west wind with its howling.

"Om mani padme hum. Om mani padme hum."

Chiseled in the granite wall of innumerable mountains, stamped upon the soul of every Tibetan child. Shouting from the fluttering prayer flags, encased in the whirling prayer wheel, murmured by millions of voices wrung dry of sorrow and hearts that long for peace.

From the cradle to the grave the life of the Tibetan is interwoven with a multitude of religious precepts and customs. When he passes a votive cairn, he adds a stone to the pile as an offering. When he approaches a *mani* wall, he never forgets to pass to the left of it. When he sees a holy mountain, he never omits to lay his forehead to the ground in homage. When a mendicant lama comes to his door, he never refuses to give him a handful of *tsamba* or a lump of butter. When he makes the round of the temple halls, he adds his contribution to the collection in the votive bowls. And when he saddles his horse or loads his yak, he hums the everlasting *"Om mani padme hum."*

The rains spent themselves, and the monsoon clouds ceased to drive across the mighty Himalayas. For half a year and more Tempu Gergan and his caravan had plodded across the mountains of Tibet. The way had been marked with suffering and fear—fear of man and gods. Across the great rift in the Indus they had struggled, and into the high hills beyond the river. And still more hills lay ahead, more valleys to cross.

They came to a pass leading to a secluded valley hemmed in by hills. Luxuriant grass, almost smothered with primulas and violets, carpeted the valley floor. A grove of apricot trees had turned yellow in the crisp autumn air. Beyond the trees the hills fell away to a distant plain which glowed with deep blues and greens. Behind them the mountains leaned icy seracs against an azure sky.

"It's beautiful." Droma gasped in delight at the lovely

valley they had stumbled into. "Tempu, must we wander forever? Why can't we settle here?"

Tempu had hoped to follow the Indus up to Leh, in Kashmir, before settling down. Leh, a trading town, would give him opportunity to trade and expand his wealth. But perhaps his wife was right. They could settle in this valley for now, as they were free of the jurisdiction of the Tibetan government. Yet around them rose the hills they loved.

Thus Tempu Gergan's journey into exile came to a close. Soon he had purchased the entire Luba Valley and established his home. Workmen erected a Tibetan nobleman's home. They built of heavy stones with a central courtyard and a guarded gateway. In a side valley a family priest cared for a little Tibetan temple, making daily offerings of rice and barley cakes to the gilded image of Sakya Muni above the ornate altar. When the winter snows melted on the passes across the mountains, wandering lamas strayed down to the valley and joined the service in the temple. Blowing on their human thigh-bone trumpets, they summoned the gods to their worship. The wind ceaselessly turned the great *mani* wheel on the roof of the temple so that its prayers spread out like a benediction over the valley. Still, brooding over it all, remained the eternal fear of the gods and dark demons of the underworld who bided their time to inflict more suffering on the family if they should fail to fill the bowls of holy water before the idol in their home. Thus passed over twenty years.

Tempu peered anxiously at his wife as she lay in a darkened room. A wizened midwife from the village far below moved noisily around the room. With obvious displeasure she ordered Tempu to leave them alone. Better that he should burn incense before the family god than to sit there fretting.

"Be careful of my son," Tempu whispered as he retreated into the sunlight. "We have waited many years for an heir."

The cry, lusty, piercing, and long, aroused Tempu from his pacing in the courtyard. "Surely it is a son; no girl would ever cry like that!"

"You are right, sir, it is a boy." The midwife peered out of the room where Droma lay admiring her new son. "You must note the time so that the lama can consult his charts."

That night the whole valley rejoiced that a son and heir had been born to the master.* They found good omens in every happening in the valley that day. A robin had twittered twice before the open window where the mother was lying. The yaks had given extra milk. These and other portents augured a happy future for the little boy.

Lamas sat before the home driving away evil spirits who might harm the boy. With the sacred thunderbolt *dhorje* they called the mighty gods to drive all demons from the valley. Then, with swinging drum and votive bell, they called kindred spirits to guard carefully the new life. At the temple they made liberal offerings to the gods for blessings on the home.

---

* The date of the son's birth poses a chronological problem. Tempu fled from Lhasa in 1855, and apparently his son was born in 1885. This would make Droma, Tempu's wife, older than seems likely at the birth of her firstborn. Two possible explanations suggest themselves: either the son was actually born earlier than 1885, or the mother was not Droma, but another, younger woman.

Yet, in the midst of all the festivities, Tempu was not happy. Always he pondered great questions that defied answers. If the gods were so good, why had he suffered so? What lay ahead for this son of his? Must he, too, face the suffering of mankind? Was there no escape from the weight of sin in this life? In his heart he cried out, "Oh, God, if there is a God, hear our prayers and *mantras* and give us peace."

On an auspicious day the lamas selected, the boy was to be named. They had studied his every move to see if they could find some clue to his former life, for they believed life flowed from body to body in an endless cycle. Sometimes the gods took human flesh and dwelt among men for a time. Some eighteen thousand living Buddhas were to be found throughout the land of Tibet. But this boy, they decided, was not a living Buddha.

When the long temple service began, the mother held the child. Heavy incense filled the air. The lamas' chanting lulled the child to sleep. The lamas offered prayers for the baby's prosperity and health. Finally, with a great clash of drums they anointed the boy with holy water and named him Sonam—Bearer of Good Tidings.

Wandering lamas from the land of the snows reported that the Presence had again returned to his people. For three years the throne had been deserted until the lamas declared the time auspicious for the return of Chenresi into the body of another Dalai Lama. The Oracle had gazed into a lake near the temple of Chapokri in Lhasa, where he had seen a vision of a strange home. It had peculiar upturned eaves and blue tiles. As he watched in vision he saw a child run out of the home. A voice cried, "There is Tendu, the Presence."

The vision faded, but immediately men set out to find the strange home with the tiles. For a month they searched the land until one day in the eastern part of the country they saw the home just as the old Oracle had described it. As they watched, they saw a little boy run out of the home. "There he is!" they cried.

The Tibetans took care to carry out the prescribed tests to prove that the child was indeed the incarnation of Chenresi. On each shoulder blade they found the small mole where the extra arms of Chenresi had been shed as he entered the human shell. On the left arm they found a birthmark in the shape of a tiger, final proof of Chenresi. Now he was enthroned in the sacred city. No one then predicted that one day he, too, would die in his youth as had the ninth, tenth, and eleventh Dalai Lamas.

Tempu rejoiced at the news, but it opened up again the wound of his exile. What happy days he had enjoyed caring for the last Dalai Lama. But here he was cut off from most of the things that gave meaning to life. Was there to be no release from the wheel of life, with endless birth and death? From tens of thousands of voices in myriad monasteries across the land the people prayed for light and peace. Would it ever come?

4/Knocking on Iron Gates

"One step farther and you will die, white man," warned the Tibetan soldier. "No one passes this place into the land of the snows. Go back to your own country. We don't want you here!"

Two Moravian missionaries found their way barred by fierce Tibetan soldiers who looked more like brigands, with long, unkempt hair which fell to their shoulders, partly concealing large silver rings dangling from their ears. They were dressed in sheepskins with the wool inside. Their right shoulders were bared for quick action with their weapons. Across the front of their loose robes they carried swords two feet in length, ancient guns, and ammunition pouches with powder and shot. They eyed the missionaries with obvious displeasure.

"But we have Chinese passports to enter Tibet. Look!"

"Our master, the *ponpon*, has forbidden any to cross this pass. The *Devashung* in Lhasa forbids any foreigner to enter the land of Tibet. Your Chinese passport—we do not want it."

"We also have an important message for his holiness."

"No! You must leave now." The soldiers cast covetous eyes on the two men's baggage.

The two men gazed over the Jelep-la (the pass) into the Chumbi Valley of Tibet. Would they never be permitted to enter the land of their dreams? They knew God had commissioned them to go to the roof of the world to help these people bound in superstition and fear. For almost two years they had tried to penetrate the forbidden land.

Dr. A.W. Heyde, the elder of the two, was determined to take the gospel to Tibet. That spark had been born in his soul years before in sunny Bavaria, as he read the story of Odoric, a Capuchin monk who had reached Lhasa and established a mission. Odoric had described the Tibetan religion as being much like the Roman religion: "In this city of Lhasa dwells the Obaysam, that is to say in their language, the pope. The monks love to gather together as our cloister people. They do not marry, and the young ones sing chants, clear, loud, and expressive after our style. Their temples are like our churches but finer and better adorned. There is an image of the mother of god, and the priests hear confessions, have holy water and a sprinkling compared to baptism."

As Heyde read, he seemed to hear a voice saying: "You must tell them about Me." He never doubted that God had thus laid on him the burden of Tibet.

His companion, Mr. Pagel, had the same conviction of a divine mission to the land where gods are mountains. While not of the same robust physique as Dr. Heyde, he made up for this with a dogged determination that nothing could crush. The two had met providentially while traveling on the same boat to China.

They had first attempted to penetrate the closed doors of Tibet from Tatsienlu (now Kangting, western China). Starting out with high hope, they reached the Kumbum monastery with its thousands of monks. Not far beyond this spot they were set upon by a fierce band of Gorolocks, who plundered their caravan and left the men for dead. Dazed and bleeding, they crawled back to Kumbum and finally to Tatsienlu, where they gradually recovered.

"Why not enter Tibet from India?" some had suggested. "There are good roads over the Himalayas from the plains of India."

Sailing to Calcutta, they journeyed up the Brahmaputra River, which north of the mountains is Tibet's Tsangpo. Again they succeeded in crossing the Himalayas, but were soon discovered and driven back across the border.

Eventually they arrived in Darjeeling, a hill town under the shadow of glorious Mount Kanchenjunga, guarding the way into the forbidden land of Tibet. From here a regular mule trail led over the deep Tista Gorge to Kalimpong, across into Sikkim, and finally to the Jelep-la through the Himalayas. Then the trail dropped into the Chumbi Valley and wound down through Gyangtse and Shigatse to Lhasa.

The missionaries enjoyed a magnificent walk through a

rain forest which filled the Tista Valley. Sweet-scented orchids hung in clusters from giant salwood trees, as gorgeous butterflies played hide and seek among them. At night the jungle echoed with the roar of the tiger and the snarl of the leopard.

They had selected this route, not for its scenery, but because they hoped the Jelep-la Pass would not be guarded as carefully as other routes. With their heavily laden coolies they had struggled through the forest and forded the treacherous Tista River. With bursting lungs they had struggled to the top of the high pass. Now it seemed that all their effort was lost. They tried to reason with the soldiers, and even offered them money, but in vain.

"If only we could enter the Chumbi Valley we would reach our goal." Pagel looked beyond the soldiers to the hills of Tibet. But one of the soldiers interrupted his musings, pointing angrily back down the pass.

"Well, Pagel," suggested Heyde, "our welcoming committee is getting impatient. We had better start moving. But we will yet succeed in bringing God's light to this land, and not all the demons of the mountains or hell will hold us back!" He motioned to the terrified coolies to pick up their loads and begin a reverse march down the trail.

The trip back would have discouraged men less determined than Pagel and Heyde. The two men talked of only one topic: Where would they try again? Just below the pass they came to a *mani* wall covered with the usual cryptic letters. Pausing, they again studied the Tibetan characters carved in the rock. Doctor Heyde exclaimed impatiently, "There it is again. The same mystic phrase of

Tibet. If only the Word of God were translated into Tibetan, the people could read the gospel for themselves."

Pagel nodded. "They say about a third of the Tibetan men can read—they spend some time in monasteries where they learn. Thousands of homes could have the Bible!"

"We must learn the language as soon as possible." Dr. Heyde looked again at the ancient *mani* wall. "It is not going to be an easy language."

As they plodded through the jungle, they discussed this new idea. Now they needed to find an educated Tibetan who would teach them the language. "That will be our first task once we get into Tibet," said Pagel. "Where do we go from here?"

"Let's try crossing through Nepal. If that fails— But we must not fail!"

Back at Darjeeling the men made a short trek up Tiger Hill to see if they could spy out a new route across the mountains. Below them lay a mist-filled valley. Across the valley stretched the long barrier of snowy mountains. Kanchenjunga loomed into the sky, dominating the scene. Farther away they could see other icy peaks—Tendong, Makalu, and even Mount Everest at a great distance.

"What a view, doctor! Have you ever seen anything as beautiful as these mountains? How can anyone see all this and not believe in God?"

"It's a marvelous view, but those mountains are what stand between us and our goal. To think that there are three million souls over there who have never heard the gospel.

"I had hoped we might go through Nepal, but I hear the

Rana rulers have forbidden foreigners to enter their country. Our only hope it seems is to go to the west of Nepal, to Naini Tal, and follow the pilgrim trail to Badrinath and then on to Kailas, the holy mountain, in Tibet. In fact, why don't we disguise ourselves as pilgrims?"

Mr. Pagel laughed. "I can just imagine you in a dhoti, doctor. You would look priceless. But who knows? Maybe it's worth a try."

They journeyed across northern India. At Naini Tal, disguised as two Bengali *hakims*, they set out on the pilgrim trail to Badrinath. Neither of them knew more than a few phrases of Hindi, nor did they know the simple customs of the people. At the first pilgrim checkpoint their experiment ended in failure. A Sikh officer sympathized when he heard their story, but he told them their only hope of success was to move farther west into Kashmir and across the Indus River into Tibet.

They trekked over more hills and valleys of northern India, finally arriving in the town of Leh, overlooking the Indus River. There in the evening light, the lingering sunset glowed blood red over the eternal snows of Tibet's mountains. Their goal was in sight, and they longed to be on their way.

"You will never cross into Tibet from here." The local governor looked again at the passports he held in his hand. "We have the strictest instructions to let no one pass this way."

"But why? Surely your jurisdiction is only over Kashmir, not Tibet," replied Dr. Heyde.

"This is true, but we dare not anger Tibet by letting travelers cross from here. I am sorry, gentlemen. You will have to forget the idea."

"We won't be beaten," said Heyde as they left the governor's office. "If the main route is closed, let us travel east along the Indus and cross by a lesser known pass. It's our last hope."

They had traveled a week when they stumbled upon the Luba Valley, where Tempu Gergan and his family had settled. Their reaction was similar to that of Droma when she had first seen the valley. It was no longer virtually empty as when the first fugitives arrived. In the center of the valley stood Gergan's home with prayer flags fluttering from the roof. From the small temple boomed a great trumpet and clashing cymbals as the lamas prayed to their gods. Tibetans in colorful clothing harvested in golden rice fields. Beyond, the snow-capped mountains marched across the land of Tibet.

"What a glorious scene!" Pagel halted his horse on a knoll near the southern end of the valley. "I wonder who owns that home?"

"It looks quite imposing," replied Dr. Heyde. "In fact, I would think the owner is a man of great importance. Let's find out."

With the best Tibetan hospitality Gergan welcomed the two men.* He offered them large cups of steaming butter tea served in exquisite porcelain cups nestling inside silver bowls inlaid with coral. Everywhere the men noticed evidences of culture and luxury.

"So you plan to go to Tibet? I don't think you will ever get there. The government is determined to keep foreigners out. Even if you did get through yonder pass, it is

---

* Heyde and Pagel arrived in Luba Valley about 1858.

many months of hard traveling to reach Lhasa. Long before you get there you will be seized and thrown back over the border."

Dr. Heyde gazed into the glowing charcoal brazier. "What do we do, then? We cannot go back."

"Why don't you stay here for a while?" offered Tempu Gergan. "Many Tibetans now live in this valley, and you can help when sickness comes."

"Would you help us learn your language better and help us write our Holy Book in the Tibetan language if we stay?" questioned Pagel.

"But yes! Surely I will be happy to do that," replied Gergan.

"Then we will stay here."

As the men lay down to sleep that night, they gave thanks to God, whose providence had led them into this beautiful valley. With Gergan to teach them and help them translate the Bible, they would see their dreams fulfilled.

5/The Valley of Decision

Years passed, and another spring came to the valley. After cool, crisp nights, the days sparkled like new wine. In the clear air the mountains lifted their snow-clad peaks like alabaster set in the clasp of the azure sky. Morning mist clung to the forest trees and snuggled under the eaves of the houses. From the temple came the aroma of incense and the murmuring of lamas at prayer.

As the sunlight swept into the central home in the valley, Sonam Gergan, nearly seven years old, stirred in his pleasant half-dream world. An illusive idea slipped in and out of his consciousness. Then he remembered. This day was the first day of *Losar*, the New Year festival. There would be visiting and dancing and, best of all, a great feast. At the thought of the feast he came fully awake. In his mind he savored the delicacies his mother, with the servants, would prepare. He wondered what gift his friend Wangchung, who lived in the next valley, would bring him. He had fashioned for Wangchung a beautiful hunting horn, made from a yak's horn. What fun he would have with Wangchung!

Just then a servant came into the room and pulled the covers off the bed. "Come on, Sonam. You must not sleep more. Today we welcome the year of the Water Dragon, and there is much to do. Your father is waiting to take you to the *gompa* to make an offering to the gods."

"All right, Choni. I'm ready."

Choni smiled indulgently as Sonam smoothed down his long black hair and wrapped his *chuba* around his body.

With a saucy nod to Choni, Sonam hurried down the stairs to where his father waited.

"Good morning, Father. I am ready now to visit the temple."

They walked with the servants to visit the temple, where the lamas had already begun their ritual of ridding the valley of the demons of the year of the Iron Hare, and welcoming the friendly spirits of the year of the Water Dragon. Periodically, clashing cymbals and the beating of drums punctuated the prayers.

Arriving at the temple, Sonam and his father passed clockwise around the building, turning each of the 108 great prayer wheels set around the temple. As they entered the temple, they passed between magnificent *thankas*, great painted banners depicting man on the wheel of life surrounded by the legions of hell. From the burning butter lamps incense rose in clouds, which floated slowly past the golden images on the altar. The golden image of Sakya Muni stood serenely under the altar's rich brocades.

As the worshipers placed their offerings of barley cakes and rice before the images, the old priest smiled happily. He seemed especially content that Tempu Gergan, his master, still worshiped the gods of the mountains and was teaching his son to honor the gods in the true tradition of Tibet. The old priest had been angered when Gergan had allowed the foreign devils to bring their strange religion to the valley.

"May the gods of the year of the Water Dragon deal kindly with you," he murmured as Tempu bowed his head to receive the touch of the holy water. "And may your son follow always the ways of the gods."

Sonam listened gravely while performing the ritual, yet somehow he felt it was wrong. The white men in the valley had become his friends, and he loved to sit on their laps and hear the stories of their God. He especially enjoyed the story of the boy David, who fought with a bear and a lion while defending his father's sheep. What a brave man David was to fight the giant Goliath with a little sling! Sonam chuckled to himself as he thought of the story again. In his mind he was David going out to meet Goliath. He thought of how his father sat with the white men day after day trying to put into Tibetan the story from their Holy Book. Yet his father had never accepted this new way of salvation they talked about. He admitted that Jesus could have been an incarnate God, but there were many such gods in Tibet. Why should they accept this new way when every Tibetan knew that only the turning of the wheel of life brought salvation?

Sonam's wandering thoughts were arrested by the great image before him. Could those golden eyes really see? Could those ears hear his prayers? His thoughts frightened him. He must not listen to that voice that kept telling him these gods were not true. The gods would be angry. As he heard the old priest whisper his name, while talking to his father, Sonam listened intently to hear the conversation:

"The boy will soon be seven, and he must be initiated into the mysteries of the faith. I am glad the white men have not corrupted him."

"You need have no fear of that. We treat them as true friends, but their religion is not for us. Sonam will always follow the way. Is it not so, my son?"

Sonam nodded; yet the questions would not leave his young mind.

Back in the home, servants prepared the feast under the watchful eyes of Sonam's mother. The years had dealt kindly with her; she still retained the beauty which had made her the envy of the women of Lhasa. Now dressed in her finery, decked with pearls and gold, she looked like a queen. Her hair had been plaited into many braids woven onto a towering head board. Through the raven hair gleamed jewels of coral and turquoise set in filigree work. From her neck hung an enormous silver amulet inlaid with gems. The amulet contained an image to Buddha, printed prayers, and a lucky charm. Over her brocaded *chuba* she wore an apron of rainbow colors. Sonam felt sure his mother was the most beautiful woman in the world.

The music of flutes and the throb of drums announced the arrival of dancers, who swept into the courtyard and slowly circled it. The men wore baggy pantaloons and multicolored jackets, with long tassels swinging from their waists. The girls wore blouses with enormous sleeves that hung almost to their knees when they stood, but waved like giant butterflies when they danced.

Heyde and Pagel arrived at the house and presented a New Year's gift wrapped in a white scarf. The family welcomed them warmly and invited them to watch the dancers. It was a colorful scene, with bright new bunting around the courtyard and the dancers pirouetting in the center. Over the scene fluttered new prayer flags. Now two sword dancers appeared on the scene. They were dressed in dark cloaks with broad white cuffs. Two yellow scarves trimmed with red ran across their chests. Each of them wore on his head a richly ornamented helmet. The two warriors bounded across the courtyard brandishing drawn swords in one hand and holding small decorated drums in the other. Most of the evil spirits which, in the opinion of the lamas, had taken up abode in the courtyard, were hastily routed by fierce blows from the warriors' swords.

Next came two lamas dressed in colorful cloaks with stag-head masks over their faces. They also carried swords, as they represented the Tibetan god of death who judges all souls during the New Year festival. As the tempo of the music increased, the stag dancers leaped high into the air, driving out any spirits the warriors might have missed.

Sonam sat entranced, listening as his father explained

the significance of each dance. Next they saw a shaggy
yak prancing into the courtyard. The men beneath the
hide skillfully copied the movements of an old yak. A
man appeared with a whip, which he cracked over the yak
as the drummer picked up the beat. With a roar the yak
reared up and waved his head from side to side in time
with the music, then lowered his head and charged the
onlookers, who retreated laughing. Now all the dancers
appeared together with the men and women in their rainbow costumes weaving in and out between the flashing
swords of the warriors, while the stags of death pranced
before the angry yak.

"Impressive, don't you think, Pagel? This year they
have gone to more trouble than usual. Remember how
Gergan reacted when he first heard of a way of escape
from the wheel of life? It was while we were translating
the verse in John, 'I am the way, the truth, and the life.'"
Dr. Heyde paused and looked across the courtyard to
where Sonam sat with his father. "All this superstition
worries me, for I know that underneath the glitter there is
a longing for something better."

"You are right, doctor. Gergan confessed to me one
day that for years he had been looking for a way of escape
from the law of Karma. He seemed happy that he had
found a new way, but somehow the moment of decision
slipped by. He seems determined now to follow the old
religion and to take Sonam with him."

Dr. Heyde looked across at Sonam again and found him
intently watching them both. "I still have hopes for
Sonam. He still listens to all we say."

For ten days all work stopped in the valley as the people celebrated *Losar* with feasting and visiting. Then they returned to their normal occupations.

Heyde and Pagel wondered whether they would ever finish the task they had set themselves to do, as it had proved so incredibly difficult. Yet they knew they must keep trying even though so little progress had been made. One of the problems was to know into which Tibetan dialect they should translate the Bible. If they used the Lhasa dialect which Gergan spoke, it would not be understood well in the east. If they used the eastern Amdo Tibetan it would be of little use elsewhere. Whichever language they used, some would not grasp the story of salvation through Christ.

To complicate things still further, three different levels of language were used in each province: the lower level for servants, children, or animals; a second level for those equal in status; and a third used in addressing officials and the living Buddhas or *rimpoches*. After consideration of all possibilities they had decided to use the classical language used in monasteries and known throughout Tibet. As many of the lamas had returned to lay life, the translators hoped these would understand the classical Tibetan. Whichever language they used, some would not understand. But the classical seemed the best choice.

Sitting down before a glowing brazier, the men warmed their hands over the embers. They glanced around the now familiar room, admiring again the tapestries and curtains. One wall was taken up with an enormous bookcase containing the sacred books of Tibet. The Kanjur consisted of 108 volumes; and the Tanjur, 235 folios. Every one of the thousands of pages had been laboriously printed from wooden blocks kept in the Kumbum monastery in eastern Tibet. The Kanjur, written in pure classical Tibetan, guided the men as they worked.

Gergan picked up the few pages they had translated from the Gospel of John. "It is not clear, my friends. You seem to be able to tell me what you want, but how can we put that into my language? You do not understand our way of life, or what words mean in our language."

Dr. Heyde nodded in agreement. "Never did I imagine anything would be as difficult as this. We thought we would merely tell you what we wanted and you would give us the Tibetan word." He fingered slowly the pages in his hand. "There must be some way to make this clear."

Slowly he began to read the first verse of John, "In the beginning was the Word, and the Word was with God, and the Word was God." He paused.

"This word 'God'—are you sure, Gergan, that you have given us the best Tibetan word?"

"Surely it is," replied Gergan. "Every Tibetan knows what that word means."

"But," interrupted Mr. Pagel, "does it not also mean the supreme Buddha, and is applied to the Dalai Lama?"

"Yes, that is right. As I have said many times, this Jesus is one of the great Tulkus or incarnate Buddhas who came to live with men. In fact, as I read this book written by John, I see Jesus as Avalokitasvara, the Bodhisativa of compassion."

Dr. Heyde sighed. Could he never get this son of the mountains to understand that Jesus Christ is the only true God, made flesh to dwell with men? Every Tibetan read-

ing the translation would pause on that word 'God' and
see the Dalai Lama on his throne, or a guilded idol in the
temple. Gergan was right: the meaning was not clear. For
two hours they struggled with the task of translating a few
more words into this difficult tongue. If only they knew
the language better or if Gergan understood Christianity
more, they would make more progress. They battled superstition and frustration. At times they wondered if
Gergan was trying to confuse them, but they decided this
was not so. The Tibetan just didn't have the answers.

Mr. Pagel turned to the doctor. "Not much progress today, doctor. Do you think we will ever finish this task?"

"It will be a miracle if we do. Somehow this language
is so confusing. Take that discussion about God. Surely
there is a word that means the one true God, but what is
it? Then we speak of prayer. For them the word means a
repetition of abstruse formulas and mystic phrases handed
down from ancient times. We speak of 'sin,' but to them
sin is a crime like the killing of animals."

"A few days ago," replied Pagel, "I came across a nomad furiously murmuring prayers while slaughtering a
yak for food. I am sure that if he could have managed it
he would have spun his prayer wheel at the same time."

"It's a strange religion with a strange language," agreed
Dr. Heyde. "All we can do is pray for wisdom."

Sonam had sat beside the men listening intently. He
was impressed by the story of Jesus. That a god would
leave Paradise and come down to earth he could understand—the Tibetan religion was built around that idea.
But there was something different about Jesus. No
Buddha had ever died on a cross to give eternal life to his

followers. The Buddhas taught a man where escape from the wheel of life lay, then left him to accumulate sufficient merit so he could escape. Sonam picked up the Gospel the men had been translating, and slowly spelled out the words.

"This is hard to read, Father. Will you be able to make it simple enough for all to read?"

"I doubt that is possible, Son. Classical Tibetan is a difficult language, but it is the best we can do. Can you read the story?"

"No, it is too hard, but I do like to hear the story of Jesus. One day I would like to be His disciple."

A frown clouded Tempu's face. "Ah, no, Son. We can never forsake the faith of our fathers. We can help the men translate their holy book, but we can never be Christians."

The days stretched into weeks and years as Dr. Heyde and Mr. Pagel struggled on with the translation of the Gospel of John. They had been joined by Dr. Jaeschke, an authority on Oriental languages. Tempu Gergan still helped them all he could.

At last they finished the Gospel of John and had it printed at Kyelang, in Kashmir. Now they had a message Tibetans could read. They arranged with a passing trader to take a yakload of the Gospels into Tibet and distribute them to monasteries. Sonam, as excited as his friends, hoped that many would read about his Jesus.

Tempu Gergan had been ill for some time, and his condition grew worse. Making a long trip to Leh, he had run into bad weather with unseasonable sleet and snow.

When he had struggled home, he suffered from a raging fever and a hacking cough. Dr. Heyde diagnosed tuberculosis and did what he could to relieve the old man's suffering. But it was obvious that the elderly Tibetan would not live long.

Sonam was now twelve years old. He watched his father slip into unconsciousness and wondered again what lies beyond this life. Surely the missionaries were right when they spoke of God's Paradise. But his father, a Buddhist, could only look forward to countless lives with more suffering and death. How he wished his father would accept Christ.

The servants, knowing their master would soon leave them, called in the lamas. These priests chanted over the sick man, striving to drive out the evil spirit that afflicted him. On a slip of paper they printed *"Om mani padme hum,"* which they pulped up in a little water and forced down the dying man's throat. Finally, in the year of the Fire Bird (1897), Tempu Gergan died.

For many days the valley people mourned the passing of a great man. Droma his wife was heartbroken and, feeble in health, seemed destined to follow her husband soon. Sonam grieved deeply, but he had a calm assurance that everything was in God's hands.

After a time the normal pace of life resumed in the valley. Sonam now declared openly that he had determined to follow Jesus Christ as his Lord and Master. Later that year he made a public profession of his faith by being baptized as a Christian in the swift stream that flowed through the valley. The lamas, of course, were horrified.

"What will you do now, Sonam?" his friends asked

him.

"My name is no longer Sonam," he replied. "When I was baptized I received my new name—Yoseb [Joseph]. God has a work for me to do, and that is to give legs to the Bible, that it may run into Tibet and tell my people about Jesus."

The missionaries, of course, told Yoseb that they felt greatly rewarded for their efforts. However, the Gospel they had struggled for years to produce had fallen far short of their hopes. They discovered that so few could read classical Tibetan that the work was practically wasted. The lamas could recite the language in their holy books, but seldom understood what they were reciting. Could it be that God had called Yoseb to translate the Bible so that it could be understood?

Yoseb heard of the benefits of education in the outside world and begged his friends to send him away to school. The missionaries gladly granted his request and sent him to the Christian Missionary School in Srinagar, the capital of Kashmir. He proved to be a brilliant student, learning both Urdu and English among other things. When he was a young man of twenty-three, the British Raj offered him a lucrative position in public service, but he refused.

"I have given my life to the Lord Jesus Christ," he explained. "If His messengers are not allowed to go to my people, I will devote myself to translating the Bible so that it can have legs and go into Tibet."

6/The Lama and the Key

Back in his little valley after several years of study, Yoseb Gergan reveled again in the quietness and beauty of the mountains.

Wangchung, dressed in his great Tibetan cloak and colorful boots, met Yoseb upon his return.

"Greetings, Wangchung. The years have been kind to you."

"And to you also, Yoseb. Welcome home. There is to be a great feast tonight to honor your return. Now we will see life in the valley again!"

Yoseb looked at the familiar sights—the home, the temple, the thatched cottages, all still there as he had known them. But the years had brought subtle changes. It was more than the thickening moss on the south of the houses or the little trees that had grown taller with the years. There seemed to be an undefinable loneliness over the valley, as though the heart no longer lived.

The impression lasted only a moment. It was quickly dispelled by the exuberant welcome he received from his old friends and servants. Everyone talked at once. Yoseb felt his heart drawn to his people, and he determined he would never forsake the valley again. First he would settle down; then, when his estate was in order, he would resume translation of the Bible.

Soon after the death of his father his mother had also died, leaving him sole heir to the family fortune. He returned home as master of a prosperous estate. Why not settle down and enjoy life for a few years? he wondered. Surely the Lord would understand that he must take time to arrange the affairs of his estate. Later he would take up the Bible translation work. Yet had not God called him to a specific task? His estate had been managed well while he was away, and he could continue as its owner. The battle raged on in Yoseb's mind.

His missionary friends had long since left the valley and moved to Leh, to the northwest in Kashmir, where they established a small Tibetan church. Over the years they had continued to work on the translation of the New Testament, but their efforts met with little success. Reports about the Gospel of John, translated at such a cost of time and effort, were most discouraging. Particularly in the east and at Darjeeling no one appeared satisfied with the Gospel. Few could understand classical Tibetan, and the actual translation was not clear. The missionaries urged Yoseb to come to Leh, pastor the Tibetan church, and help with the Bible translation. The decision he now faced: Should he stay in the Luba Valley or go to Leh?

One night Yoseb dreamed. He saw a mule caravan laden with goods coming over the pass into the valley. He could hear the mule bells ringing in the clear air, and the shouts of the muleteers. To Yoseb's amazement they unloaded the mules at his door. What a treasure they carried—jade ornaments from China; priceless wood carvings from Nepal; woven wool mats from the Chumbi Valley of Tibet; costly garments and other exotic treasures. The leader of the caravan waved his hand, exclaiming, "These are your treasures, master, and more are yet to come."

Yoseb suddenly recognized these as his own men. A mule had moved close and was breathing down his neck, so he instinctively reached out his hand to push the mule away. His hand grasped the swinging shutter over his couch, through which the morning air was blowing.

The movement woke him completely, but so vivid was the dream that he could hardly believe it was only a dream. What did it mean? As a Tibetan he believed every dream had a message, but what was the message in this one?

As he lay thinking it through he fell asleep and dreamed again. A few Tibetans sat in a humble church listening as the minister read from a great volume spread out on the desk. Leaning closer, Yoseb was amazed to see that it was a Tibetan Bible. The pages were written in letters of fire. The man preaching seemed shadowy and indistinct, but the voice was his own! Looking around, he saw the little group listening with close attention. Now the voice spoke again: "Which way will you choose, my friends? One way offers wealth and luxury, but no hope of eternal life. The other is hard, but leads at last to a golden city with joys forevermore."

Yoseb awoke from his dream and pondered the message. God had spoken—of that he had no doubt. Slipping to his knees, he asked God to forgive him for his covetous spirit. Life in the valley would lead to great riches, but that was not the way God wanted him to go. As soon as possible he would leave all this behind and join the struggling band in Leh.

He divided the great estate among the servants who had cared for it through the years. When all was settled he rode out of the valley headed for Leh, leaving his old life forever. He crossed a broken, twisted landscape, forded foaming mountain streams, climbed over steep passes.

Occasionally the torrents were "bridged" by structures that required a keen eye and strong nerves to negotiate. Many were no more than two hand-woven ropes of cane planked over at intervals by boards of doubtful integrity. These structures tended to gyrate when the traveler reached the most vulnerable spot in the center, threatening to throw him headlong into the foaming river below. Still more terrifying were the chasms crossed by a flying-fox apparatus. The traveler sat on a sliding block that shot down the dipping rope at a frightening speed till stopped by the ascending rope on the other side. From there he hauled himself hand over hand up the steep rope onto the opposite cliff. The mules and loads were strapped in turn to the ingenious contraption and laboriously hauled the last few yards to safety.

In spite of the difficulty of the journey the scenery lifted his spirits to God, who he felt was leading him forward. Only a great and powerful God could create these magnificent hills and clothe them in such white beauty. Yoseb took in the scene with mixed feelings. Beyond those crags lay some 3,000,000 souls to whom Jesus was unknown. If only he could cross those mountains and share his Saviour with the people! But this would have to wait. The lamas and monks would never allow it. In God's good time the door would open, and the Bible would be the wedge.

The missionaries warmly welcomed Yoseb Gergan. "God be praised! How good you look! We have waited long for this day." Dr. Heyde held Yoseb's hand warmly between his. "We feared you might decide to stay in your lovely valley."

"That was a great temptation, my friends," Yoseb admitted. "Only your prayers have helped me give up my valley to work with you here. I can never thank you enough for all you've done for me."

"You have nothing to thank me for, Yoseb. God has been with you and has led you back to us. If only our old friend Pagel could be here to see this day, he would share our joy. But God has called him to his rest. I have prayed that I might live to see this day, and God has been good to me. As you can see, the years have taken their toll, and I can no longer carry the burden of the work."

"You will not leave us then, honorable father?" Yoseb gazed anxiously at his friend, aged and stooped from years of toil.

"No, Yoseb, I will not leave you, as I have decided to

stay here until the Master calls me to lay down the task. My only home is in the glory land."

The two men moved around the mission compound, meeting the personnel of the Tibetan mission. "Yoseb, you must meet Dr. H.A. Francke, our chief translator." Dr. Heyde paused before a room where a scholar sat surrounded by piles of manuscripts. Seeing the two men at the door, he sprang up and came to them.

"So this is Yoseb? How much I have heard about you and your burden for your people in Tibet. Dr. Heyde never tires of telling me what a brilliant scholar you are. Welcome to Leh!"

Yoseb knew instantly that he and Dr. Francke would be good friends. The man had a warm smile and friendly eyes that showed genuine pleasure at meeting the newcomer.

"Dr. Francke is one of the world's leading authorities on Oriental languages," said Dr. Heyde. "Already he has become an expert in Tibetan. You will get along famously with him, I am sure."

"Now, doctor, not too much back scratching please! Yoseb will get the idea that we have all the answers, but you know how difficult our task is."

The little Tibetan church welcomed their new pastor. Here was someone they could talk to in their own tongue. "You see, Yoseb, there is plenty to do here," remarked Dr. Heyde.

"There is more than I expected. First of all I want to read the manuscript of the Bible and see how the work is progressing."

Dr. Francke and Yoseb sat down to check over the

translation work. "You see, Yoseb, we have here the Gospel of John that your old friends prepared. This translation was never a success. It does not give the true meaning to the Scriptures. Later Dr. Jaeschke came and spent some years trying to revise the translation. But his death stopped further effort."

"Yes, I have heard about Dr. Jaeschke. Did he ever find the key to the translation?"

"No, I don't think so. Our work so far has not been very successful. I have been working on a complete revision of the New Testament. The first translation made at Kyelang did not turn out well, as you know. The classical Tibetan is difficult to translate, yet we seem to have nothing better to try. I want you to take my revision, read it carefully, and tell me frankly what you think of it."

As Yoseb read the manuscript, he agreed that this was still not what they needed. Clearer than the earlier translation, it was still defective though Dr. Francke had tried so hard to put the gospel story in clear Tibetan. If he had failed, what could Yoseb do more? Falling on his knees, he pleaded with God to give him wisdom.

For weeks the men toiled together, with mounting frustration. Early one morning Yoseb set out on a long walk to visit some Tibetans in a valley north of Leh. By midmorning the heat had become intense, and the panting hiker sought a place where he could rest in the shade. Ahead he saw a little Tibetan temple with a stone seat against one wall. Thankfully he sank down on the seat and idly listened to the monk inside as he chanted and turned the great prayer drum almost twice the height of a man.

Suddenly Yoseb sat up eagerly as the meaning of the lama's words registered on his mind. Could it be true? The lama was reciting from some ancient book that seemed to contain the very phrases the translators had searched for. Rushing into the temple, Yoseb begged to see this strange book.

"Walk softly before the gods, my son," the monk admonished. "Haste and passion are the sins of youth, but the flesh must be subdued."

"My apologies, honorable one, but I would see the book from which you read."

Reverently the old lama lifted the faded pages for Yoseb to see. "You ask whence comes this book? Only the gods know. My father read from this book, and his father before him. It was written by the gods themselves."

Yoseb smiled to himself but did not dispute the origin of the book. Sitting down, he began to read the tattered pages. As he read, his excitement grew. The book told of ancient wars of the gods, with a backdrop of superstition. But the language, written in a dialect almost forgotten, amazed Yoseb. He saw at once that this language was the key for which they had searched. Here was the word for "God" which they had so diligently sought, a good word for "prayer," and other difficult phrases. The language, much simpler than the classical Tibetan, could be adapted so that the modern Tibetan would understand it clearly— even the simple people of the hills.

But how could he secure this book, so that he and Dr. Francke could study it more carefully? Never would the lama sell his holy books. Yoseb knew better than to offer money; instead he must appeal to the old man's heart.

"My friend, never have I heard sweeter language than this. Today my soul has been mightily stirred by this book of yours."

The old lama nodded quietly. "I can see the stirring of your soul as you have read the pages. It is good. The wheel of life turns on, and brings every man to his destiny. Today the gods desired that you should hear these words."

"Honorable one, I serve the great God of heaven whose name is written in these pages. Never have I seen this before. What merit would be yours if you would allow me to share these words with my friends. Will you let me take this book and read it to them? In a few days I will bring it again."

Eagerly he watched and silently prayed, as the old man pondered the strange request.

The lama looked long at the book before replying. "Never have I allowed another to touch that book. It has been a treasure carefully guarded. No stranger could ever take my book—and yet, somehow I feel you ought to have it. I do not know why I do this, but I want you to take the book and share it with others. Soon my spirit will escape from this shell, and there is no one to take these books from me. Take it, my son, and may the gods be with you."

He gathered the worn pages and tied them between their leather covers. Handing it to Yoseb, he again entreated him to care for the old book.

Yoseb could scarcely refrain from shouting for joy. This was far more than he had ever hoped for. The book was his to keep. "*Tutiche* [Thank you]! The book will be carefully guarded. And may the great God of heaven remember your gift."

Forgetting his trip to the hills, Yoseb rushed back to share the book with Dr. Francke.

"This is wonderful, Yoseb." Dr. Francke read slowly from the faded pages. "God has led you to find this book. We must start today to rewrite the New Testament. With our new key we shall bring the people God's Word in the Tibetan language."

Yoseb Gergan
Photo courtesy of British and Foreign Bible Society

7/In Perils Oft

Yoseb read newly translated selections from the Bible in the little Tibetan church. Now the words came alive; they stirred the listeners to a new devotion to God. At first he had planned to translate only the New Testament, but with the newfound key the whole Bible could be translated. Why had neither he nor his father thought of using this language? Why had so many years been wasted, when the answer at last proved so simple? Yoseb pondered the question but never found the answer. He could only conclude that God works out everything in His own good time, and he must be content to leave the matter there.

Yoseb Gergan toiled on for years in the work of translation. Even with the key before him, sometimes he spent months interpreting a single book of the Bible. Dr.

Francke returned to Europe, but while he lived Yoseb kept in touch with him.

At last, in the Tibetan year of the Wood Hog (1935) Yoseb laid down his pen. Now fifty years old, he had toiled since he was twenty-three with the stupendous task. Gazing on the completed manuscript, he bowed his head: "Thank you, Lord. The task is done. Now the Bible has legs to go to my people. Now the Book will be printed; then it will go to its appointed task. May it be soon, Lord."

Reverently he picked up the thick pile of manuscripts from his desk. Here was the hope of a people beyond the snows, who had never heard the good news of salvation. Soon they would hear and understand.

Yoseb stared unhappily at the letter in his hand. Again he read the words, "We are sorry, but we have no way to print a Tibetan Bible here in India. We suggest you send the manuscript to the British and Foreign Bible Society in England. They will be able to do the work you want." The letter's writer represented the Bible Society at Lahore, where Yoseb had hoped to have the new translation printed. To England! So far away! Could he let his precious manuscript travel over the great ocean? Yet, what other hope did he have?

He packed the pages which had cost a lifetime of toil and sent them away. Then he waited to hear that his precious package had arrived safely.

The arrival of the Tibetan manuscript at the Bible Society in Britain generated a wave of excitement. Tibet, that closed land of mystery, was at last to have a Bible of her own! Eagerly the staff gathered to see the parcel opened.

"Which way do you read it?" questioned Shirley, a secretary in the manuscript department. "Do you begin at the back like Chinese and read the words in columns?"

"How would I know?" answered her friend Sue. "It looks hopeless to me."

The secretary of the society smiled. "I cannot read it either, girls, but I do know it is like most of the Indian languages. This means you start at the front of the book and read across the page from left to right. We will have the manuscript carefully checked before it is printed."

First they compared the manuscript with Tibetan texts in the British Museum. Travelers to Tibet had collected these books over a period of years, and the Younghusband military campaign to Tibet had yielded some of the volumes.

Securing the aid of scholars, they had the manuscript laboriously copied. Then they prepared a list of questions. They sent the manuscripts with the questions to the Tibetan borderlands of China, and to Bhutan, and Sikkim, small Himalayan kingdoms with substantial Tibetan populations. The reaction to the Bible by the Tibetans in Sikkim proved of special interest, as this kingdom is a gateway to Tibet from the Asian subcontinent of India. At that time over a thousand mules a day plodded over the Nathula Pass bringing the exotic treasures of Tibet—gold, silver, furs, and yak tails. Returning, they carried kerosene, clothing, and other items.

In Sikkim the manuscript was tested around campfires each night. Skilled researchers carefully read from the

Bible, then questioned the muleteers about the scripture they had heard. To their delight the Tibetans understood the translation.

Bhutan boasted a number of centers of Tibetan learning. One of these, the Tiger Lair Monastery, clung to the side of a precipice. Here Tibetan scholars agreed to examine the Bible portions to see if they were in clear Tibetan. As the old lamas read the pages, they seemed ready to adopt it as one of their holy books. "This is an inspired book," exclaimed one of the *rimpoches* (living Buddhas).

These words and others like them echoed along the borders of Tibet. The survey committee finally reported to England, "Never would we have believed a Tibetan text would be so readily accepted by the diverse Tibetan peoples. We look forward to the final preparation of this inspired translation."

Back in Europe war threatened. Adolf Hitler's Panzer divisions goose-stepped across the Austrian border and later threatened Czechoslovakia. Britain prepared for war. The staff of the Bible Society, worried about the valuable manuscripts in their vaults, began to arrange for their dispersal to safer centers.

In September, 1939, Hitler invaded Poland and the world was at war. Germany smashed Poland and then turned to crush France. Next Hitler ordered his bombers to pound the British into submission. The hail of bombs fell on the cities, reducing many areas to smoking rubble.

The Tibetan manuscript lay in an underground vault of the Ripon Cathedral, 200 miles north of London. As the Battle of Britain reached its height, enemy bombers moved farther north, and places previously thought to be safe received their share of the bombs.

One 2,000-pound missile from the skies landed on a roadway beside the Ripon Cathedral and came to rest against the wall of the church without exploding. Four feet away, inside the church's wall, lay the Tibetan manuscript.

Gingerly a bomb demolition crew defused the bomb. The firing device seemed faultless; so they could not understand why it had failed to explode. The old sexton was certain that a divine hand had sabotaged the bomb.

By the time the nightmare of the Great War had ended, Yoseb Gergan was sixty years of age. He wrote anxiously to Lahore, asking when the Bible would be printed. Was he not, before he died, to see this book to which he had devoted his life? If the Bible could not be printed in England, could the Bible Society return the manuscript to India to be printed there? The Lahore Bible Society had acquired new equipment and felt that the work could be done there. They requested London to return the manuscript to India, and the request was granted.

When the manuscript reached Lahore, the printers looked at the closely written pages and shook their heads. "We can never print from that manuscript. It has been written on cheap Tibetan paper which has not taken the ink well. We have no Tibetan type, so we had hoped to photograph the manuscript and print by the lithograph process."

"I am afraid we cannot use this copy," explained the press manager. "Our only hope is to have the manuscript rewritten on special white paper so that we can get sharp photographs. But we cannot buy such paper at present. I suppose, however, we could secure the best paper possible and prepare the surface with our own chemicals."

Chandhu Ray, the Bible Society secretary, looked at the tattered manuscript. "Are you sure you know how to prepare the right chemicals?"

"With God's help I am sure it can be done," replied the manager. "At least it's worth a try."

They treated thousands of sheets of paper with chemicals mixed with egg yolks and were highly pleased with the results. Now the task was to write the Tibetan text carefully on the sheets. Who would be able to do the writing?

Yoseb, learning of the problem, begged the Society in Lahore to send the Bible back to him for rewriting. It would be a tremendous undertaking, but at the same time he could make some necessary corrections.

The Lahore Bible Society sent the manuscript on its perilous journey, which included long distances by mule-back. Finally it reached Yoseb at Leh. Holding the manuscript again in his hands, he felt his old enthusiasm return. He set to work immediately revising the text and writing it in Tibetan ready for the press.

Days and months slipped by as Yoseb concentrated on the exacting task. Two years passed, and still the work was far from finished. The aging Tibetan felt his strength ebbing, and once or twice he suffered from dizzy spells. Would he ever finish the rewriting?

Then it happened. As he sat writing on his low table a searing pain shot through his chest and down his left arm. He fell unconscious to the floor. His servants rushed in to find him breathing feebly and gasping for breath. They lifted him gently up on a bed and called a doctor.

"Poor fellow; his heart has given out," said the physician. "There's very little hope, I'm afraid."

Members of the little church in Leh believed God would never take their beloved pastor until his work was finished. Who else could complete the Tibetan Bible if Yoseb died now? They gathered around the dying man to plead with God to spare their pastor. The devil must not win the contest now.

God must have heard their prayers, for Yoseb slowly regained his strength till he could sit up in bed. Then with a specially prepared table he resumed work on the manuscript.

"I ought not to let him work like this," said the doctor. "He may live five days or five months. Who knows? There is a fire burning in him which keeps him alive."

Two Tibetan scribes, Gappel and Phunthsog, now did most of the writing, leaving Yoseb to check the written sheets. But time was running out. They needed more help; so they found two more scribes, Stobldan and Zodpa, to help finish the task. Each man had his distinctive way of writing, so that the finished manuscript bore five different styles.

There were days when Yoseb could barely hold the sheets passed to him. With willpower and dependence on God, he determined to see the task concluded. The work became a race against death. Would he last? And if he failed, who else could do it?

Now there was no time to rewrite a page if a mistake was made. Correct it as well as possible and press on! James, the epistles of Peter and John, Jude, Revelation—

still Yoseb nodded approval as each page was finished.

Then came the day, August 11, 1946, when Yoseb Gergan read in Tibetan the words: "Surely I come quickly. Amen. Even so, come, Lord Jesus. The grace of our Lord Jesus Christ be with you all. Amen."

"Thank You, Lord," whispered the old warrior. "Come quickly. My task is now finished. This Bible will speak to the millions of Tibet."

Five days later, in the Tibetan year of the Fire Dog, Yoseb Gergan fell asleep in his Lord.

8/The Case
of the Terrified Courier

The manuscript was now ready, but as yet the Tibetan Bible was not produced. The sheets were taken from Leh over steep mountain trails to Lahore, where the Bible Society prepared to complete the printing. They placed transfers on thin plates and put them through little "rocking" machines so that impressions could be brought out on white paper. The first set of proofs revealed a number of faults in the manuscript, and all agreed that one of the Tibetan scribes who had worked with Yoseb Gergan would have to make the corrections.

How would they get the proofs to Leh? The best plan seemed to be to dispatch them with a special courier who knew the mountain trails. Their search finally led to a pleasant young Tibetan, Sandrup, who owned a sure-footed mountain mule. After the usual bargaining the two parties agreed on a price, and the Tibetan started his difficult journey. The journey to Leh would take him some fifty days with equal time to return. He would also spend some time in Leh. He promised to return in four months with the corrected proofs to Lahore.

Days turned to weeks and weeks into months while the Bible Society waited anxiously for its precious proofs. What had happened to their courier? Had he fallen among bandits or been caught in the war? Of one thing they were sure. He had never reached Leh where Gappel, the Tibetan scribe, anxiously waited for the proofs. What should they do now? All normal routes into Kashmir had been closed, and no mail was getting through by regular channels.

Chandhu Ray, Secretary of the Bible Society, called his staff together. "Our first effort to reach Leh has failed, but we must not give up. We have already prepared another set of proofs, but we do not know how to get them through to Leh. Do you have any suggestions?"

"Could we not post them?" suggested one young man.

"No; it's too uncertain. Every day there are fresh outbursts of violence, and many mail bags have been destroyed."

"Then our only hope is to send another courier through the mountains."

But how could they ask another man to face the unknown dangers of the mountains? Finally the old caretaker, Badi, spoke up.

"I know just the man to do the job for you. He is a Pahari, a man of the hills who will succeed if anyone can.

Besides, he is a Christian."

"Let's ask him," Chandhu Ray concurred.

Bahadur willingly offered to take the proofs to Leh.

"You know you will face many dangers?" Chandhu Ray asked him.

"I know it will be difficult, but I know the mountain trails. And am I not a follower of Isu [Jesus], who will protect me?"

So with the prayers and good wishes of the Bible Society staff, Bahadur set out to follow the steps of the previous courier.

Each day before dawn he loaded his mountain pony and climbed along the treacherous trail. In the late autumn he had little fear of avalanches, but nights on the high trail were bitterly cold. Thoroughly familiar with the mountains, Bahadur was able to take a more direct route than the previous carrier and to avoid the villages in the valleys.

The trail lay over one of the most beautiful alpine areas in the world. In the distance gleamed the white seracs of the great Himalayas. The hillsides flashed scarlet and gold with autumn tints against the deep green of the coniferous forests. Far below, like golden handkerchiefs, fields of ripened grain gleamed along the valley floor. The grandeur of the hills spoke to the traveler of the love of God. With a prayer for protection and guidance he set his face toward the high passes ahead.

The distant goal came gradually closer until one final pass lay between him and his journey's end at Leh. The weather had been kind to him on the trail; he had passed through only occasional mild rains. Light snow fell, now that he was in the high altitudes, but real winter weather was yet to come.

As Bahadur and his horse climbed higher, Bahadur noticed thick clouds boiling up out of the valley far below. Then a freezing rain began to fall. He had no fears, however, as the trail was well defined and he was warmly clad.

But as he neared the top of the pass, an eerie silence prevailed in the mountains, except for his own labored breathing and the clopping of the horse's hooves. In the distance the silence was broken by the echo of thunder as a storm passed over the next valley. Then he heard it: the rising whine of wind and rain as the storm blew up the far side of the pass.

The man and his horse reached the top just in time to catch the fury of the storm.

Pulling his horse behind a sheltering rock, Bahadur squatted down, waiting for the storm to pass. The sleet had turned into egg-sized hailstones pelting the terrified horse. Suddenly there was a searing flash of light followed by the crash of thunder. The horse tried to bolt into the darkness, but Bahadur restrained it with tremendous effort.

Flash after flash of lightning glanced off the rocks around them, filling the air with the heavy smell of scorched earth. The thunder roared as though the demons of hell had gathered to defy the terrified traveler. Torrential rain followed the hail, pouring from the heavens like a waterfall.

Bahadur lay in terror against the heaving belly of his horse. Never had he seen a storm like this. He felt the hair rise on the back of his head. It seemed in the darkness as if fiendish hands stretched out to drag him off the mountain. He imagined he could hear the demons' muffled laughter.

"Oh, God," he cried, "help me now. Deliver me from Satan and his evil host. Protect Your Book!" His shouted prayer was answered by another flash of lightning, which laid him out insensible on the ground.

When consciousness struggled back, the storm had passed. He noticed that all was quiet, and he suddenly realized he was stone deaf. His horse stood by, held by reins fortunately twisted around the man's wrist. Staggering to his feet, he lurched down the trail to the town far below. It would be weeks before he would hear a sound, and then only faintly, as the storm had split his eardrums. At last he reached Leh and plodded along the little town's main street looking for the Christian chapel and the Tibetan scribes who lived next door.

News had reached the scribes that proofs were on the way, and they welcomed the bedraggled Bahadur. Finding him stone deaf, they led him to a low seat while they removed the pack from the horse. Eagerly they unfastened the saddlebags and reached in to pull out the proofs. With a startled cry Gappel, one of the scribes, jumped back. *"Ari Bhai!* What has happened here?" He upended the saddlebags, and soggy masses fell on the floor.

Bahadur cried out in dismay. The storm had done its work well. Water had filled the saddlebags, reducing the paper to pulp.

Bahadur tried to unpick the sticky mess, but it was no use. His journey had accomplished nothing. He called

God to witness what the devil had done to the precious papers.

9/The Persistent Scribe

When the news of what had happened to Bahadur and the proofs reached Lahore, consternation reigned at the Bible Society. Now they felt sure they grappled with something too big for human beings to handle. The whole church must entreat God for protection and help in printing the Bible. They sent letters to Christian churches throughout India and to friends across the sea, asking them to pray for completion of the Book.

"It reminds me of the time when the devil tried to destroy the Bible in France," Chandhu Ray told the group of workers in Lahore. "During the French Revolution the Bible was banned in France, and on one occasion a Bible was tied to the tail of an ass and dragged through the streets. The people also kindled huge bonfires to burn

Bibles. But they never succeeded in annihilating God's Word. Even in England the devil used to try to stop people from reading the Bible, but he failed. If the church will now pray to God, I'm sure the devil will be defeated again."

So they prayed. In the chapels among the great mountains; in the bamboo churches in the tropics; in city cathedrals and in Christian homes throughout India, in public and in private, a plea arose to heaven for help to finish the Book. New hope came to the workers in the Bible Society. They would try again, and with God's help this time they must succeed.

Fighting had died down in the mountains; so it was decided to send a third set of proofs by regular postal service to Leh. There would be a risk, but would it be any worse than those already taken? With prayer they committed their papers to the post and awaited the results. By truck and horse and speedy courier the package sped on its way over the hills of Kashmir. Armed guards escorted the mails through bandit-infested hills. Finally the mail reached Leh. With jubilation the scribes opened the package and found the papers intact.

Gappel, the scribe, was overjoyed. Now he could quickly make the necessary corrections and send the proofs back to Lahore. Sitting down at a low table, he started work on the sheets. Before long he realized that the master manuscript would need certain corrections and alterations before the work would be perfect. But they would never send the original translation out of Lahore—not in these troubled times. He recalled the fury of the devils on the mountaintop and shuddered again as he thought about the hapless Bahadur. Only a few weeks ago travelers had found the skeleton of the first courier in a deep valley. He had evidently been caught in an avalanche.

"Somehow this work must be finished in spite of the devil's attempts to stop its being printed," said Gappel.

His wife came over to inspect the progress of the work. "Soon you will be ready to send it back to Lahore." She picked up one of the pages and again admired the neat handwriting of Yoseb Gergan. "The old man had a wonderful hand. Look at this writing!"

"There is more than beautiful writing there," commented Gappel. "Only a genius or a man inspired of God could have made that translation, and I think Gergan must have been a part of both."

"What will you do when you have finished the corrections?" Gappel's wife flicked through the pile of papers on the table. "Will they be able to make the corrected version in Lahore?"

"That worries me. It needs the touch of a Tibetan hand." He sat musing for a while; then he had a flash of inspiration.

"That's it! I will take the papers back to Lahore myself and stay there until the printing is completed."

His wife was appalled. "No! You cannot do that. Have we not heard that new fighting has broken out and the whole country is in turmoil? How could you leave us here and die on the way to Lahore? No, you must not go." She broke into loud weeping.

"What is the matter?" cried her sister who lived with them. "Some calamity?"

"Gappel says he is going off to Lahore. He will meet the army on the road and be killed, and what will happen to all of us?"

"You know," Gappel explained, "how much we long to have the Bible in our own tongue. It is no longer safe to send these papers back through the post. And even if they do arrive in Lahore, who will correct the master copy? There is only one solution. I will have to go to Lahore and do the work myself!"

The Christians in Leh prayed for wisdom to know what they ought to do. They knew that unless the Bible could be printed soon, it might never be completed. Any day they might be caught in the war. At last they decided that Gappel should take the proofs to Lahore and stay until the Bible was finished. Gappel's friends asked him whether he felt he could find his way through the mountains.

"My friends," he replied, "it is many years since I first met Yoseb Gergan. I was a Buddhist youth, following carefully the religion of my fathers. I lived as an acolyte in Sera Gompa in Lhasa, and I was trained to copy the sacred books of Tibet. Those were hard days for a boy. We arose long before dawn to join in prayers in the great hall. After a breakfast of *tsamba* and butter tea we began our studies for the day. Always there was the round of the monastery images, where we made daily sacrifices of parched rice and butter. How we boys dreaded entering one room where fearful demons hung on great banners around the walls! In the dim smoke they seemed to come alive and breathe out fiery hatred as we came near. How careful we were to make sure we presented our offerings properly!

"We spent hours reading and writing. If one of us made one small mistake, the monk tutor pounded us with his great cane. I tell you, we learned to write carefully with teachers like that."

Gappel noticed that his friends smiled. "You may smile now, but it was no joke for a small boy far from his home."

"Why did you leave the monastery, Gappel? Did you tire of the life there?"

"Not really. An uncle of mine was coming to Kashmir and needed someone to accompany him. He begged the old abbot to let me go, assuring him I would enter another monastery when we reached Kashmir. What a trip that was! It seemed so wonderful to leave the smoke-filled rooms of the huge monastery and be free in the hills again.

"When we reached Kashmir, I entered the little *gompa* at the other end of the town, where I continued my study to become a Tibetan scribe. It was there that I first met Yoseb Gergan. Many evenings when the day's work was done he would come to the monastery and talk to us about his God, Jesus. We wanted to argue with him, but he never seemed to notice. When we protested that there are many gods and Buddhas in the world, he pointed upward and asked, 'Who made the snow-clad hills and the stars of heaven?'"

"One night he persuaded me to come down to this chapel and listen to him speak. Never have I heard a more wonderful sermon. It seemed as if every word was just for me, and I went home a troubled man.

"Before long the love of Christ touched my life, and I joined you here in worship."

"Well do we remember that night," Paulus, the old elder, smiled at Gappel. "We had prayed for many weeks that you would follow the light, but our faith was weak. Only Yoseb seemed certain you would forsake your old ways and join the new way."

Gappel nodded. "It was a great struggle, but never have I regretted that decision. Later when I was called to work with Yoseb in translating this Book, I knew God had called me. All the training of my youth prepared me to be a tool in His hand that His Word might speak to our people.

"You ask me if I think I ought to go to Lahore and whether I will ever get through. Brethren, this is no time for such questions. God's Word must be finished, and the only way to finish it is for me to go to the city beyond the mountains. Whether or not I succeed is not the important thing. To follow God's will is more important."

"May God then go with you," said Paulus. "Let us gather around our dear brother and commend him to God for the perilous journey ahead."

The Christians knelt in prayer and committed Gappel and his precious papers to the care of their heavenly Father. A few days later Gappel's family and friends escorted him out along the trail toward Lahore. Somewhere beyond those hills men were dying as the armies of India and Pakistan fought for possession of Kashmir. Like the couriers before him, Gappel would have to follow the high mountain trails and avoid the troubled valleys.

A few of the stronger men followed the scribe to the foot of the first pass and there paused to say their final good-byes. "Do not fear for me, my friends. God will go with me." Gappel looked around at the familiar faces. "If anything happens to me, look after my family. I can only leave all in God's care."

"Have no fears for your family. We will see that all their needs are met until you return. Go carefully, but come again quickly with the finished Book."

Gappel led his pony up over the pass. His dangerous journey had begun.

10 / Into the Lion's Jaw

Months passed, while Chandhu Ray anxiously waited for Gappel to appear in Lahore. But man, manuscript, and horse had vanished leaving no clues. Great concern was felt for the lonely traveler, as the war had entered a very critical stage with reports of thousands of civilians being destroyed between the armies.

Chandhu Ray, of the Bible Society, called his little band of helpers together. "Again the evil one has scored a victory, but the fight is not over. Gappel left Leh almost four months ago, and no one has heard anything since. I have bad news that his wife and family are greatly concerned, and the church is praying for his safety. We, too, must pray that God will overrule. This is God's Word we are preparing for Tibet, and not all the demons in hell can prevent its being published and doing its appointed work in that country. The devil fights us so because he knows this Book will free his captives bound in superstition and fear. We must pray now that God will show who really rules this world."

Again the little group took heart and knelt down to cry to God for help. Chandhu Ray pleaded with God to protect Gappel and show them what they should do next. There seemed to be no way forward; yet he was determined not to retreat.

Later in the day Chandhu Ray heard a faint knock at the door of his study room, and a muffled cough. Opening the door, he found a beggar from the hills. Daily these poor creatures limped around town with the same plaintive whine for help. Chandhu Ray sighed. Already that day two others had come. But, strange to say, this old man made no attempt to beg.

"Who are you, my friend? Why have you come to my home?" Chandhu Ray questioned.

"Sahib, I have not come from this town, but have traveled many days over the mountains. See, I bring you a message."

From the fold of his voluminous gown he extracted a grubby sheet of paper which he handed to Chandhu Ray.

As Chandhu Ray scanned the brief message his heart leaped in surprise. It was a cryptic message from Gappel! So he wasn't dead at all. On the sheet of paper Chandhu Ray read a Bible text, "Come quickly . . . . Come, Lord Jesus. Gappel." What a strange message! What did it mean? He must know more.

"Come in, my friend." He bowed to the old man.

"You must have refreshments, and then I will reward you for your faithfulness."

The old man's face lighted up, and he eagerly followed Chandhu Ray into the bungalow.

"Ah, sahib," he began, "the whole country is going up in smoke. Everywhere there are soldiers, and they kill without mercy. The two armies are camped up by the Dras River. Soon they will cross it and fight again. The Pakistani troops are north of the river and the Indian army south of it. Never have I seen such hatred between men. It was an evil day when I was born into this world."

"Where did you meet Gappel?" Chandhu Ray interrupted. "Why did Gappel not come with you?"

"Oh, sahib, you don't understand. No one can get through the army to the south—no one but an old beggar who asks for food at the camp kitchen."

"But where is Gappel now? Is he with the Indian army? I must find him as soon as possible."

"You find him? You're a Pakistani, aren't you?"

"Well, yes."

"Then you could never find Gappel. You wouldn't live five minutes if you tried to pass the Indian army. Gappel is living in a little hut beyond the Dras River, waiting for the trails to open again."

"Why doesn't he go back to Leh to his family?"

"That is impossible, sahib. The army has closed the way north. Gappel told me how he tried to go back and was nearly shot. When he left Leh, he came up with a Pakistani patrol. In order to avoid them he made a wide detour around the mountains. When he finally rejoined the main trail, he found himself caught by a terrible bombardment. For hours he lay sheltering behind some large rocks until the firing stopped. He crept down to the river only to find Indian troops patrolling the bank. They refused to let him pass, and ordered him back to the hills. Then he found himself hemmed in between the two armies. He has been waiting there for weeks. He was afraid to write more, but said you would understand. He also said that the papers were safe, but I don't know what he meant by that."

Now Chandhu Ray knew why no word had come from Gappel. The fate of the entire Tibetan Bible lay in the hands of this man, yet he was cut off as if a prisoner on a lonely island.

"Tell me, old one, how do you cross the river? Are there boats?"

"No. There is a bridge across the river, and the bridge is guarded by a Sikh regiment. You can never cross it!"

"You may be right, old one. But with God's help I will get through and bring Gappel out to finish the Bible. This is God's work; it must succeed."

"So be it," whispered the old man. "Our fate is in the stars, and what must be will be." Picking up his reward, he salaamed and passed out into the night.

Speed, Chandhu Ray knew, was essential. How he could possibly reach Gappel he didn't know, but he knew he must try. Any day Gappel could be killed. He asked the Pakistani government for help to try to reach the Tibetan. They listened sympathetically to the story but refused to help.

"Impossible. No civilians can enter Kashmir from Pakistan. It is more than your life is worth. We are sorry."

Chandhu Ray then decided to try to enter Kashmir from India. He heard that a DC-3 air service operated between Amritsar and Kashmir twice a week, and hoped to fly in to Srinagar on the plane. He set out by train for Amritsar.

To his delight he found a flight leaving the same day he arrived in Amritsar. Taking a small case packed with Hindi Gospels and Testaments, he hurried to the airport and checked in for the flight. In ten minutes the plane would be ready to leave; it already wore a "boarding" sign. Suddenly a voice boomed over the airport speakers.

"Ladies and gentlemen, we are sorry to say this flight has just been canceled. A government order which just arrived prohibits all further flights into Kashmir. Please return to the airport lounge."

The announcement stunned Chandhu Ray. The door to Kashmir had just closed in his face. But God could open it again. Bowing his head, he prayed.

He asked the airport manager the meaning of the announcement. "Surely this order could not have been meant for today. Supposing it had come five minutes later, what would you have done? Besides, do you have the money to refund all our fares?"

The manager looked troubled. Already many of the passengers were angry with him.

"All right," he said, capitulating. "I have no money to refund all your fares, and the plane is filled with fuel. We will fly to Kashmir. If the government had wanted us to cancel this flight, they should have told us sooner. Please take your seats."

The passengers looked amazed at the sudden change.

But Chandhu Ray bowed his head and whispered, "Thank You, Lord."

The plane left behind the steamy heat of Amritsar and headed toward the mountains. On every side stretched the hills of Kashmir, while away to the east lay the great white barrier of the Himalayas. As the plane neared Srinagar, Dal Lake gleamed blue against the green fields. Yet Chandhu Ray scarcely noticed the glories of snow and forest. His great concern was how to pass the army barring his way. Only a miracle would save him from death, and he prayed for that miracle.

Once clear of the airport, he flagged down a passing truck which took him near the Indian army. Leaving the truck, he walked slowly up the road.

"Halt! Who goes there?" An armed guard stood in his way. He must be careful not to reveal his identity. "I am a Christian preacher just come from Amritsar. I have brought some books for your men to read."

The guard was suspicious, but he relaxed when he saw the Testaments.

"From Amritsar, you say? I don't have much time for your Christian stories myself, but some of the men may want to talk with you."

Now Chandhu Ray could see why Providence had led him to enter Kashmir from Amritsar and not from Pakistan. Now he was past his first barrier. Approaching a group of men standing by a campfire, he pulled out copies of the Gospel of John and passed them around. For many days the soldiers had camped by the river, bored with life. So they listened with apparent interest as their visitor told them the story of Jesus and His love for all men.

Beyond, Chandhu Ray saw another fire glowing and joined that group. He silently prayed that he might find someone to help him in his quest for Gappel. As he talked with the men, one asked, "Why did you leave the faith of your fathers to follow this Western religion?"

"My friend, Jesus was a Jew, and He came to help all men. Let me tell you how I became a follower of Jesus." Chandhu Ray told how he had been born in a poor home, and a passing preacher had sold his father the Gospel of John. That book had changed their lives. Finally he told the story of the Tibetan Bible and how the devil had tried to destroy it. Somewhere beyond the bridge lay the manuscript for that Bible.

The troops, including a ranking officer, seemed to enjoy the story, but made no move to help find Gappel. Chandhu Ray was disappointed. At last he lay down beside the fire and slept.

The next morning Chandhu Ray accepted the hospitality of the soldiers, who shared their rations with him. At last the officer looked up from his rice and curry and asked, "You say this scribe is just beyond the river?"

"Yes. I understand he lives in a hut not far from the bridge."

"Your story sounds a little fantastic to me. Suppose you go with me across the bridge and we look for this scribe. Are you willing?"

"Thank you, sir. It is good of you to help me like this."

"You know what will happen to you if you have been lying?" The officer fingered the revolver at his side. "We know what to do with spies."

"I have no fears. With God's help we will find Gappel, the scribe, and he will have the manuscript with him."

As the two men crossed over the long bridge, the sentries saluted and let them pass. Chandhu Ray knew his miracle was taking place. God had opened every barrier.

Chandhu Ray had memorized the route described by the old beggar, and soon found the village he sought.

"There is the house!" Chandhu Ray pointed to a thatched whitewashed cottage. "Gappel will be in there with the papers."

A Tibetan opened the door and peered out.

"Are you Gappel, the scribe from Leh?"

"Yes, I am. But how do you know my name?"

"I have come from India to find the manuscript of the Tibetan Bible. My name is Chandhu Ray. You are to return with me to help finish the printing of the Bible."

"Praise God you have come! I had despaired of leaving this place alive."

"And this book you have?" The officer interrupted. "Let me see it so I can be sure this story is true."

"Surely. Here it is, and while I have waited I finished all the corrections."

The officer examined the strange writing.

"So this is Tibetan. Certainly it is a strange language. Hearing the story of this Book and seeing it today makes me want to know more about it. What do you plan to do now? Can I help you further?"

"Yes, sir," Chandhu Ray replied. "Will you escort us back over the bridge and arrange for us to go to Srinagar? From there we will return to India."

"To Pakistan, you mean," the officer stated. "I heard

your name a moment ago, and all my suspicions were confirmed. An hour ago, if I had known that, I would have ordered you shot without mercy. But now I feel I ought to help you. God alone knows how you ever got this far without being detected."

Thankfully the two men followed the officer across the river to his headquarters. The men crowded around to view the strange papers and reverently salaamed as they moved away. Arrangements were made for the two men to travel to Srinagar in an army convoy soon to leave.

At Srinagar their worst fears were confirmed. All civilian flights out of Kashmir had been canceled. Roadblocks had been set up throughout the country, making it virtually impossible to travel. They were trapped.

"Surely there must be some way to get a permit to fly from Srinagar." Chandhu Ray looked again at the airport official. "Planes are still flying; so someone must be using them."

"Only the sick and wounded fly out, and occasionally those with a Priority One Pass."

"Where are these passes issued? We must see the officer in charge."

"Only the inspector general of police can issue a Priority One Pass. If he gives you the permit, we will fly you out with the wounded."

Chandhu Ray palled at the idea of approaching the inspector general. He was a Sikh, and Sikhs were renowned for their bitter hatred of the Pakistanis. If he knew who Chandhu Ray was, there would be no hope for them. Gappel was for trying to sneak past the patrols and walking through to India. He had never been in a plane and dreaded the noisy monsters. Chandhu Ray disagreed. They must try to get the necessary passes, risky though it was. After a brief prayer he decided to declare himself to the inspector general and leave the results with God.

At the police headquarters he sent through his card with his name and position clearly shown. Immediately he was summoned before the Sikh inspector.

"Are you a Pakistani?" The massive bearded Sikh at the desk glowered at Chandhu Ray. "How dare you come here like this? You are a spy and will be shot immediately. We have no Pakistanis around here."

"Not only am I a Pakistani, but I have been behind your lines to get this Book. I am no politician or spy. I am concerned about the publication of the Bible in Tibetan. See, here is the Book." Chandhu Ray showed the manuscript to the inspector and briefly told him its story. He noticed the inspector beginning to relax.

"How did you get here in the first place, and how could you possibly get past our troops?"

"My Lord has said, 'All power is given unto Me in heaven and in earth.' By His power I did it. Now we need two Priority One Passes to take us to India."

The officer glared at the two men, but thumped a bell on the table. A junior officer hurried into the room and saluted. "You called, sir?"

"Write out Priority One Passes for Delhi for both of the men." Rising quickly he saluted and marched into another room.

Chandhu Ray again bowed his head in thanks. He had seen another miracle. At the airport he showed the precious passes to the army colonel in charge.

"Where did you get these?" he demanded. "No such permits have been issued to civilians for weeks. They are forgeries! Sergeant, take these spies and deal with them!"

A burly soldier laid hold of the men.

"Not so fast, my friend," Chandhu Ray twisted himself out of the grip of the soldier. "Why don't you ring the inspector general to confirm that our passes are genuine?"

The colonel telephoned, and looked amazed. "I don't understand it, sergeant, but the passes are genuine. In fact, the inspector general said the men were to be treated with utmost hospitality."

He apologized to Chandhu Ray. "We can never be too careful, you know. A plane will leave within the hour for Delhi."

11 / Wind off the Snow

Gappel gazed uneasily from the aircraft window as the plane gained altitude. In the distance the two travelers watched as the snowy peaks of Gappel's beloved mountains grew faint in the distance. They could see peasants, far below, clustered like ants around a dried forest leaf, cultivating their fields.

"How does this great machine fly?" Gappel looked anxiously at Chandhu Ray. "Will we reach earth safely again?"

Chandhu Ray smiled at his Tibetan friend. "Have no fear, my brother. We are in the hands of God. See, we are already out of the mountains."

"Will there be trouble when we reach Delhi? I fear this dreadful war. In fact, I thought we would never leave Kashmir alive."

"I do not expect trouble in Delhi," answered Chandhu Ray. "We will go immediately to a friend's place and wait for the early morning train to Lahore."

"How clever men have become! My mule would never cross the mountains at this speed." Gappel gazed again at the ground racing beneath the plane.

The "Fasten Seat Belt" sign flashed above the cabin door as the plane dropped rapidly toward Delhi. As the plane circled low, Gappel was even more astonished.

"What an enormous city! Never have I seen such a village. Does all India live in this city?"

"India has many such cities," Chandhu Ray explained. But he saw that this was too much for Gappel to grasp.

When the doors of the plane swung open, the hot, fetid air of the Indian lowlands swept in like a blast from a blowtorch. Outside the plane the sun beat down from a copper sky. The temperature soared to more than 110°F. Even the usually raucous crows crouched listless, their feathers drooping in the heat.

Chandhu Ray watched in some alarm as Gappel gasped for air and staggered across the runway to the shade of the airport buildings. Gappel, he knew, had never known heat like this before. He was a man of the mountains who reveled in the bracing air of the winter blizzard. As the two men entered the airport lounge, Gappel began to sway dizzily, and his companion quickly showed him a seat.

"Oh, my head! I am dying. Never will I see my family again." He looked mournfully at Chandhu Ray.

"Never fear, my friend. You will not die. Soon you will adjust to the heat and be able to bear it like the rest of us."

"Never, never! Please help me." Chandhu Ray, seeing how pale and sick Gappel looked, knew he must get Gappel away at once.

Summoning a taxi, he half carried the listless Gappel out of the airport. Even the breeze that swept into the taxi as they traveled was hot and oppressive. Gappel really looked ill. By midafternoon the temperature reached a peak of 114° in the shade, with a humidity of 90 percent.

Reaching the home of his friends, Chandhu Ray placed Gappel on a mat beside an open window. The scribe's head was burning hot with fever, and the feverish man gasped for air.

Chandhu Ray looked helplessly at this friends. "What can we do? Unless there is relief soon, I fear Gappel will succumb. Surely all my efforts to bring him here are not in vain."

Chandhu Ray again felt Gappel's burning forehead. "How can we travel by train to Lahore when he is like this?"

"We can ask God to send the rain. He controls the earth and can send rain if we ask." Chandhu Ray's friend looked out at the shimmering heat across the plains. "It is two weeks until the monsoon is due, but these last few days the heat has been unbearable. I do not wonder that your friend cannot stand the heat."

"Yes. He is a man of the hills, and this is more than he can take. You are right about God's power, but it would take great faith to believe it would rain today."

"Have we no faith?" questioned his friend. "You have told us of the miracles God has already performed for you. Now we must ask for another."

The little group knelt around Gappel and pleaded with God to send relief. How God would answer their prayer they did not know, but they left it in His hands.

That evening dark clouds boiled up from the south and spread across the sky, blotting out the light of the setting sun. Shortly after 8 o'clock lightning flashed, followed by thunder. Then heaven's sluice gates opened, and three inches of rain fell on the parched earth before morning. The monsoon had come, bringing cool, damp air with it.

Chandhu Ray sat at the window and watched the rain. He exclaimed,

> "Give unto the Lord, O ye mighty, give unto the Lord glory and strength.
> Give unto the Lord the glory due unto His name; worship the Lord in the beauty of holiness.
> The voice of the Lord is upon the waters: the God of glory thundereth: the Lord is upon many waters."

"Lord," he prayed, "this is another miracle I see to-night. Surely Your hand is over this task. Lay Thy healing hand on Thy servant Gappel, and give him strength to finish this journey."

Gappel rallied toward morning and volunteered to continue the journey. Chandhu Ray decided he would get second-class seats for the trip so as to make things more comfortable for his Tibetan companion. The rickshaw soon deposited them at the station, where they were to take the train to Amritsar on the Pakistani border.

"Two second-class tickets to Amritsar, please." Chandhu Ray pushed his money across to the ticket clerk.

"I'm sorry, sir. I cannot help you. There is an army contingent traveling on the train, and all first-and second-class seats have been purchased. I have only third-class tickets, but I warn you it will be crowded. In fact, you may not even be able to board the train. Would you rather wait for the afternoon train?"

Chandhu Ray was dismayed. "If you can give us only third-class tickets, I guess we will have to make the most of it. My companion has been ill, and I was hoping he could lie down and rest. With another hot day coming on I dare not stay in Delhi."

They made their way to the platform to wait for the express train. The din on the platform resembled a mob in riot. Long before the train was due, people gathered enormous piles of bedding and luggage, jockeying for position to attack the train. Vendors of every kind shouted up and down the platform, weaving through the massed humanity—men, women, and children, with pigs and baskets of chickens.

"Garam chai, garam chai [Hot tea, hot tea]!" shouted one peddler who carried clay cups in his hands and a glowing stove on a board on his head.

"Pani, pani [Water, water]!" called the water carrier as he, too, searched for customers. When he found one he directed a thin stream of water toward the person, who caught it in his mouth. Purchasing a hand of bananas, Chandhu Ray and Gappel sat on their luggage and munched the delicious fruit.

As the train thundered at last into the station, Gappel trembled with fright. "Oh, my friend," he cried, "what strange monster is this?"

"Come, Gappel. Do not fear. This is the train I have told you about. Are not the wheels bound to the great steel rails? It cannot hurt you. It will speed us on our way. Now hurry, we must get a seat."

The waiting sea of humanity waited no more. The tide flowed toward the train even before the cars stopped. Passengers trying to exit met head on those clawing their way aboard. No one thought of forming a queue. By some magic the alighting passengers managed to pass their copious luggage to the shouting coolies and climb over the multitude fighting their way up the steps.

Many decided they must find some way other than the packed doorways to board the train. Since the large windows in the third-class compartments had no glass or bars, here was the best way to enter the carriage. The technique was as simple as it was brutal. Placing piles of luggage on their heads, the passengers rammed their way through the windows, forcing back those already there. It was a question of the survival of the fittest.

Gappel found himself pushed by the crowd toward the carriage door, and by some strange power he finally ended up inside the carriage. No vacant seats remained. Near him a thin Indian woman fought to retain her seat as a fat Bengali tried to push in beside her. "You great oaf," she screamed, "here I am sitting in a miserable thirteen inches and you push your great hulk in as well!"

On the other side a farmer dressed in a loincloth tried to push a basket of complaining chickens into the over-crowded luggage rack, but it was physically impossible.

Gradually the passengers achieved a more orderly form of chaos in the carriage. Gappel sank exhausted on a pile of luggage, overcome with the swaying of the train and humid odors of livestock and soiled clothing. As the train gathered speed, he became sick, to the disgust of those around him. Gappel was long past caring; he only hoped the journey would soon end. "Dear God," Chandhu Ray whispered, "do not desert us now, but lead us to our journey's end."

The route lay through the wheatlands of central India, but now all looked arid and brown. The monsoon was working north from Delhi, and in a few days the farmers would have their oxen out, plowing the ground for planting. There was much of interest on the 300-mile journey, and Gappel began to feel better as the day passed.

Late that night they arrived in Amritsar, where Chandhu Ray hired a taxi to Lahore. The task of rescuing Gappel had been completed, and now they could finish the translation of the Bible!

Next morning Gappel began his work on the final corrections before printing. But the day grew increasingly hot and stifling, bringing Gappel to the point of exhaustion.

"I cannot work here," he gasped. "This heat is dreadful. You will have to get someone else to help with the Bible. Please send me home."

"But you can't leave us now, Gappel. It has been so difficult to get you here, and no one else can do this work," Chandhu Ray reminded him.

"I know, sahib. I ought to stay and finish the work. But really this heat will kill me. If only I could breathe wind off the snow, I could work."

"Wind off the snow!" exclaimed Chandhu Ray. "That gives me an idea!"

Rushing to a large ice factory, he ordered fifty large

blocks of ice and arranged to have them delivered to the Bible Society office.

"Fifty blocks?" The manager looked startled. "Do you mean fifty blocks?"

"Yes, I do, and please send them quickly."

They set large tin trays around on the floor and stacked the ice on the trays. They set two large fans in position to blow on the ice blocks and provide Gappel with a man-made Himalayan breeze.

"Wonderful, wonderful!" cried Gappel. "You have surely given me the wind off the snow. Bring in the sheets. I am anxious to see the work finished."

Gappel settled himself at his table in the middle of his "ice cave" and took out the proofs he carried with him. With the corrected proofs before him he began the final manuscript corrections. As he finished each sheet, the press foreman rushed it away to prepare the printing plates. Enthusiasm spread to the entire staff. The printers kept the press rolling twelve hours a day.

Chandhu Ray stood shivering in the room where Gappel worked happily. "This place is like an icebox. I don't know how you exist here. Besides, you must rest more. You do not take time to eat or exercise."

"It is wonderful, sahib. I feel strong, and my mind is clear. A man can't think in the dreadful heat."

"Your mind may be clear, but you haven't had a decent meal all day. You must eat properly if you are to finish the work."

"Ah, sahib, you do not understand. I am not hungry when I have the Word of God before me."

"That won't keep you alive. Tell me, how long did you

sleep last night?"

Gappel picked up a sheet of the Bible from his desk. "I do not know how long I slept. Really I am not tired, and I long to see this work finished."

"I will tell you how long you slept. Five hours. The night watchmen said you were at work long before daylight. Please do rest more. We want to see this printing finished without having an invalid on our hands."

"All right, sahib. I will promise, but really you must not worry about me. I never felt better. Another two days should see these corrections finished. How long will the printing take?"

"They have already finished the Old Testament and are now starting on the New Testament. We are printing only 5,000 copies. I would like to think another two days should see the first copies printed."

Gappel worked on. His estimate of only two more days for corrections proved inaccurate, but he kept ahead of the press. Up to twenty hours in a day he worked at his little desk, sustained, he said, by heavenly power.

Then came the wonderful day in August, 1948, when the final sheets rolled off the press. The staff gathered around the bookbinder as he added the last signature to a copy of the Book. After a few hours he came back and laid in Chandhu Ray's hand the first printed copy of the Tibetan Bible.

"Wonderful!" cried Chandhu Ray. "Is it possible that after all these years we see this Book? Gappel, come over and see your Book."

"Nay, sahib, not my Book but God's Book and Yoseb Gergan's Book."

"You are right! How Yoseb would have thrilled to see this Book completed! I have just been reckoning how long has passed since Dr. Heyde and Mr. Pagel found Tempu Gergan in the Luba Valley and began to study and translate. It is just over *ninety years!* Imagine it, Gappel, that Book you hold has taken ninety years to produce. No other translation of the Holy Scriptures has ever called for such prodigious effort in time and lives."

"Why did it take so long? If God could help us produce it now, why did He not help the men long ago?" Gappel looked puzzled as he opened the heavy Book in his hands.

"That we don't know, my friend. But this we do know: God works everything out in His own time. He knows no haste or delay. One day the answer may be clear. What do you plan to do now? Can I buy you a train ticket and send you back to the border?"

"Never, sahib! You will never get me into one of those

On this page from the Tibetan Bible, John 3:16 is underscored.

machines again. If you will be so kind to buy me a good pony or mule, I will find my way back over the mountains."

"We will be happy to do that, but what about the war?" Chandhu Ray objected. "There is still strife in Kashmir."

"God has led me here, and He will lead me home. The fighting is less now, and by keeping to the high trails I will get through."

"All right, Gappel, we will see that you have what you need for the journey; but please be careful. You know what happened to the first courier we sent over the mountains. We want you back in Leh to read this wonderful Book to the people there."

They bought Gappel a horse and helped him prepare for the long journey. Then they escorted him and his precious new Book far out of the city and watched him ride toward the distant mountains.

"There goes the first Tibetan Bible on its way to Tibet," murmured Chandhu Ray. "Yoseb Gergan's dream of giving the Book legs to run to the people of Tibet will yet be fulfilled."

For over forty days Gappel pushed his horse over the mountain trails. On occasions he saw distant fires as armies swarmed over the land, but he did not meet a solider on his entire journey. Daily he read from the Book he carried and prayed that God would lead him home.

At last, weary from his long journey, he rode into Leh and made his way to the Tibetan Mission.

"Gappel has returned. Come and see!" Friends and neighbors rushed out to greet the traveler.

"No, it's not Gappel. Gappel is dead! He vanished many months ago."

"Did you not get news that I had reached Lahore?" Gappel queried. "I wrote you that I had reached safety and would return."

"No such news ever reached us. But now, read to us from God's Holy Book."

12 / Through
the Bamboo Curtain

Two thousand maroon-robed monks sat huddled in the cold, dingy chapel of the 3,000-year-old Buddhist monastery of Tra-Yarpa, which clings to a mountainside. A woman spoke to them—one who was not even a nun, but wore the robes of a Tibetan warrior.

For nearly seven and a half hours the woman spoke. At times she lowered her voice to a whisper. Then she raised it to a passionate pitch which echoed through the low-roofed chapel. Then the aging chief abbot beside her cautioned her not to speak so loudly. Chinese soldiers were less than a mile away.

When Madame Rihpiedorje finished her discourse and left Tra-Yarpa in the early dawn, she had prevailed in yet another citadel of conservatism. The Tarpa abbots agreed

to let their nuns join her anti-Communist guerilla force—
the Tibetan Women's Freedom Army.

One abbot summed it up quietly: "One of the tenets of
the Buddhist faith is to avoid violence and to trust in the
power of the gods. But as the gods have failed us, we
must take to arms."

"When the Chinese attacked our defenses in Kham,"
another added, "we felt sure they could never overrun
Tibet. We spent thousands of *sangars* and *gormos* on offerings for the gods, but all to no avail. I fear we are for-
saken, so we must support the guerillas."

So another pocket of resistance was born in the heart of
Tibet.

Madame Rihpiedorje typified many of the guerilla
leaders of Tibet, yet in one way she was unique. She was
the only woman guerilla leader with her own troops. Her
story goes back to the Tibetan year of the Iron Hare
(1951), when China decided it was time for Tibet to come
back to the "motherland." The Tibetans had memories of
the Chinese from earlier dealings and did their utmost to
save their country. Not only would their whole life be
changed, but Chinese atheism would crush their religion.

All over Tibet the people flocked to monasteries to invoke the power of their gods. They placed great faith in
magic and strange portents that appeared throughout the
land. It was rumored in Lhasa that the lamas had invented
a huge prayer wheel which could fly through the air.
Around the edge of the wheel were many knives that
would mow down an army as the "flying saucer" swept
through them. While many did not believe such rumors,
they trusted implicitly in their gods. Thousands gathered

before the temples to swing their prayer wheels and pray for deliverance.

Near Chamdo in eastern Tibet, where the red dragon was preparing to leap forward, the smoke of costly incense rose day and night from the temple altars. Cymbals clashed and priests chanted endlessly. From the hills of Kham the Khamba nomads flocked into the town of Chamdo.

Each was eager to receive the blessing of the abbot and to receive the sacred charms that would protect him in battle. One swarthy Khamba warrior swaggered over to his companions and pulled out from under his shirt a string of bags containing sacred relics. "If my heart is pure, fifty bullets can't kill me. This is a powerful charm that I wear. Let the dogs come, and I will deal with them!"

Another produced a "magic" stone from a pouch at his waist. "This also is a mighty charm blessed by the *rimpoche* at the Kumbum monastery. No steel can enter my body while I wear this!"* None scoffed at this statement.

As the Chinese soldiers marched in, these warriors rushed boldly into the battle believing in their charms and their gods.

And the Chinese mowed them down!

"We are doomed," cried the Tibetans. "Our gods have failed us!"

Madame Rihpiedorje watched with horror as the soldiers surrounded the fort defended by her husband and a

---

*The author on one occasion was giving injections to a group of Khamba refugees. Three times he plunged the needle into one man's arm only to find the skin like stone, which bent the needle. The Tibetan suddenly remembered that his "magic" stone was still on his belt, so he removed it and handed it to a friend. One the next try the muscle was soft as cheese and the needle went in smoothly!

handful of picked men. Suddenly the Chinese blasted down the door and stormed onto the flat roof, where they overpowered the Khamba warriors and hurled them over the parapet to their death below.

Grief-stricken and angry, Madame Rihpiedorje took to the hills to join the guerillas. The Khambas had been notorious bandits for generations, subject to no one except that they maintained a filial devotion to the Dalai Lama. Now as they saw monasteries burned, gods destroyed, and their wives and daughters ravished and slain by the conquerors, they swore vengeance on every Chinese who crossed their trail.

Soon Madame Rihpiedorje collected a group of reckless women around her—the beginning of the Tibetan Women's Freedom Army. Their feats of daring were legion. The Chinese commander of Lhasa received a message that seven Red soldiers had been done to death ninety miles south of the capital, and "all the bandits are women!" A letter the bandits left behind read, "We will return again and again until Tibet is free." It was signed "Rihpiedorje."

The ambush was followed by more deadly blows at Communist lines of supply and communication. The Women's Freedom Army's stock of captured Russian arms steadily rose.

On one of her forays through the high country, Rihpiedorje first saw the Tibetan Bible. Wondering what strange book this was, she took it to her hidden camp in the hills. Beside the campfire that night she read for the first time about the God of heaven who made the sun, the moon, and the stars. As she gazed at the stars above her, she pondered whether a God might live up there. The only god she knew was the Dalai Lama, and his life was threatened continually.

Night after night by the flickering firelight she read the old story that was new to her. How she longed for an end to the killing and strife. As she read more, she began to think about this Jesus who came down to live with men. What kind of God would die on a cross? She wished someone could explain it to her.

"Love your enemies, bless them that curse you, do good to them that hate you, and pray for them which despitefully use you, and persecute you." The words seemed to leap out of the page and point a finger at her. *"Love your enemies"?* Love the Chinese who had murdered her husband and defiled the temples? Never! She would fight on until she died or the enemy was driven out of the land!

But the seed had been sown and nurtured. Would it one day yield a precious harvest?

A gray-brown cloud of swirling sand enveloped the Norbulingka, summer abode of the Dalai Lama at Lhasa. It was the evening of March 17, 1959, in the Tibetan year of the Earth Hog. The Dalai Lama had received a curt note ordering him to come to the Chinese camp without his attendants or bodyguard. Such a command was without precedent and aroused the fears of the cabinet who felt he should not accept. The Dalai Lama finally agreed to go if his cabinet of six ministers could go with him. The Chinese reluctantly accepted this provision.

However, news of the note leaked to the crowds in Lhasa. The city swarmed with monks and Khambas who had come for the Monlam festival. For months tension had been rising between the Tibetans and Chinese, with guerrilla activity intensifying. Hearing of the Chinese demand, the people of Lhasa were further angered. Thousands of chanting Tibetans swarmed around the Norbulingka, refusing to let anyone out. Fearing treachery, they would not permit the Dalai Lama to go to the Chinese camp. The crowd elected leaders to organize them into fighting units. Some were armed with sticks or slings, while a few possessed ancient rifles. Some of the Khambas owned old machine guns of doubtful integrity.

The Chinese readied their artillery around the city to force the Dalai Lama to obey their summons. The Dalai Lama still hoped to placate the Chinese. He begged the people to let him go, to save bloodshed. But they refused. The final breaking point came when the Chinese lobbed two mortar shells into the Norbulingka. The crowd went out of control, screaming at the Chinese to go home and leave Tibet for the Tibetans.

Advisers appealed to the Dalai Lama to flee before the Chinese captured him. They called in the leaders of the crowd to seek their help.

"Will the Holy One leave the city now?" they inquired.

"I shall go," he replied, "if by going I can help my people and not merely save my life."

The delegation prostrated itself at the god-king's feet, imploring him to leave at once.

"Your holiness must go before it is too late!"

Sunlight shone on the courtyard and filtered through the trees of the Norbulingka parklands. The god-king, accompanied by his mother, sister, brother, cabinet ministers, and others, made ready to leave. But how could such a large party pass through the Chinese lines? they wondered. That evening a windstorm swept through Lhasa, enveloping the Norbulingka in a curtain of swirling sand and dust. Visibility was reduced to a few yards.

In small groups the escapees crept out through the gate, which had been cleared by the leaders of the crowds. They left behind most of their belongings, as speed was vital. Disguised as a soldier, the Dalai Lama slipped out of the palace and mingled with the crowds outside. Crossing the river in waiting coracles, the party formed on the other side and rode furiously for the hills.

Over twenty hours passed before the Chinese discovered their prey had flown. Then in fury their artillery opened up on the city, destroying temples and palaces. They reduced the Norbulingka to a smoking ruin and badly damaged the great Potala. Five thousand Tibetans died in the hand-to-hand fighting that followed the shelling. The Chinese seized the remaining officials, threw them all into prison, and then executed many of them.

The Chinese did not know which way the Dalai Lama had gone, but suspected he had taken the direct route through Gyangtse and Phari toward India. Khamba guerillas cut the communication wires, and this added further confusion. The Chinese sent out aircraft and troops to intercept the Dalai Lama, but failed to find him.

Rihpiedorje and her women warriors had played a leading part in getting the Dalai Lama's party to safety. Taking their position with the Khamba bodyguard, she and her followers fought a rearguard battle with the Chinese, delaying them until the Dalai Lama's party crossed the

Tsang-po River into Khamba-held territory. Later she also escaped to India, where she learned more of Christ and accepted Him as her Saviour.

Day by day the Dalai Lama's party followed rough, stony tracks through the mountains of southern Tibet. They heard reports of a great Chinese manhunt ranging over Tibet. The Chinese, they learned, expected the Dalai Lama either to stay in Yatung, southwest Tibet, or to head for Bhutan. The Lama did neither, but headed for the nearest crossing to India in the Assam Hills.

The weather took sides with the Dalai Lama. For most of the eleven days the party traveled over a vulnerable trail from Tsetang to the Indian frontier, thick clouds covered the mountaintops, hiding the fugitives from Chinese planes. And then—strange but true—the day after the party reached safety in India the clouds lifted and the sun shone clear and bright. The lamas accepted this as the answer to their prayers to the gods who control clouds.

In India the Buddhist community, including other Tibetan refugees, received the Dalai Lama with a tumultuous welcome. His two brothers had already fled to India and had gone on to the United States of America. Many other important Tibetans had found refuge in India and were trying to establish a new life.

At his new home in Mussoorie the Dalai Lama gazed wistfully across the great Himalayas. Reports carried by tens of thousands of refugees told of hardship and unspeakable atrocities committed against the Tibetan people. Whole villages had been wiped out. When the invaders discovered that the men had fled to join guerilla bands, they killed the women and children. They forced thousands of monks into slave labor, to build the highways crisscrossing Tibet. Even worse to the Dalai Lama, the Chinese destroyed the people's religious symbols and broke down their altars.

Did no one care for his people? The great nations would not stand against China, but stood back while the slaughter continued. What hope remained for the people of Tibet? Had their gods abandoned them?

At this time Christian missionaries presented to him a copy of the Tibetan Bible.

"Tutiche [Thank you]!" exclaimed the Dalai Lama. "I have heard about this Book, and have seen it only once before. That was when I was in Kalimpong during the Buddha Jayanti celebrations in 1958. Unfortunately I did not take it back into Tibet, and left it behind. I have wondered what happened to it. I am told that it speaks of the great God who became a man and lived on earth. Of course there are many such men in Tibet."

"That is true about Jesus' coming to this earth," replied one of the Christians, "but, more than that, it tells how He broke the bands of death and returned to heaven. He is now preparing a beautiful home where there will be no more suffering and death, but life evermore. One day soon He will return to earth and end this terrible trouble."

"May He then come soon," murmured the Dalai Lama. On at least two occasions he promised actually to read the Bible.

More refugees poured over the pass and into the Indian town of Kalimpong near the Sikkim-Tibetan border. Thirty thousand crowded into camps that dotted the hills. Many were wounded and desperately sick. Many families had lost father, mother, or children as they fled. Orphans roamed the streets searching for food. Various organizations supplied relief food daily, enough to maintain life. But the refugees needed healing of body and healing of mind.

Daily the medical van nosed its way into the camps and over to a monastery where the sick came by hundreds to find relief. From morning until late at night a procession of Tibetans with fevers, ulcers, toothaches, and other ailments came to get the help they needed. As many as 200 patients a day sat waiting their turn to see the "doctor," actually only a nurse. To each patient he gave a portion of Scripture from the new Bible, and wherever possible he presented the complete Bible to a Tibetan who seemed especially interested.

Each night the refugees sat before a screen and viewed full-color pictures of creation and the life of Christ. The Tibetan preacher spoke fervently of the great God of heaven who sorrowed over His suffering children. He painted a word picture of the eternal home which could be theirs. No longer, he urged, need man believe in being bound to the wheel of life, revolving through countless rebirths to reach the tree of life. Jesus had opened a new and living way into the land of eternity. From the Tibetan Bible he read the words of life.

Daily in the marketplaces and mule camps, Bibles were presented to traders who promised to take them beyond the mountains into the forbidden land. Then as they stopped to trade or to worship at the temples, they would leave behind the Bible or portions of it.

In the secret recess of a temple cell in the sacred city of

Tashi-Lhunpo an old monk sat reading the Bible before a charcoal brazier. "Surely these are great words," he said to himself. "Never have I heard such a story as this."

Taking up his pen, he dipped it in black ink and wrote in beautiful flowing Tibetan:

"Dear unknown friends, The book you have sent over the mountains has come to my lonely cell. My soul has been strangely stirred as I have read these words. Light has come to my poor darkened soul. Please send me more light."

A Tibetan trader carried the letter over the mountains and down to Kalimpong, where Christians gave the Bible to all who would take it. As the missionary read the letter from the old lama, he thanked God again for the Book that could pass into the heart of the forbidden land and speak in temple cells. He pressed Tibetan tracts on a trader and begged him to take them back to the old monk at Tashi-Lhunpo. As he watched the Bible-laden mule climb over the pass, he prayed that God might permit their safe arrival.

A Communist general in Lhasa, tired of trying to communicate across the language barrier, decided to learn Tibetan, and ordered his officers to learn it also—fast! But they lacked textbooks. How would they learn?

The only book in both Chinese and clear Tibetan was the Bible, and somehow the Chinese commander knew this. He secured Bibles confiscated from Chinese Christians, and copies of the Tibetan Scriptures, and set his officers to studying them. And so across Tibet the conqueror opened the Book of God to learn the language of the people. They found there the words of life that speak to the hearts of all men whether Chinese or Tibetan, rich or poor, conqueror or slave.

Along the "bamboo curtain" of Tibet many people received the Word of God. Their own gods had miserably failed them, offering no way out of their suffering and despair. What they needed was a God who could help in time of need. And as they read, some found the hope for which they searched. Around the campfires the Book spoke to the lowly nomad about the divine Shepherd searching for His lost sheep in the hills of Tibet. In nobles' palaces it told of the great wedding feast to which all men were invited.

Now it seemed less obscure why God had permitted the years to roll by before the Bible could be translated and printed. When priests and lamas ruled a closed country, few Bibles could have entered the forbidden land. Copies would have been seized and destroyed, while those who carried them would have faced probable death. But now deep tragedy had overwhelmed Tibet. Monasteries were destroyed, the people subjugated, monks conscripted for slave labor. When hope in men and gods had been wellnigh destroyed, at this precise time God's Book appeared and spoke to the people of peace and life and hope.

In the valleys and mountains of Tibet, in darkened temple cloisters, in hermits' caves, far beyond the din and bustle of life, now the voice of God, through the devoted pen of His servant, Yoseb Gergan, speaks words of life to His suffering children.

God has given "legs" to the Bible that it may run into the land of Tibet, telling all of the God who "so loved the world."